W9-BML-342

The Polymer Clay Artist's Guide

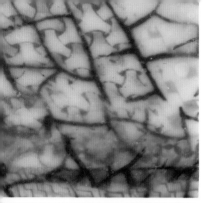
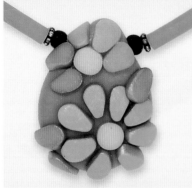

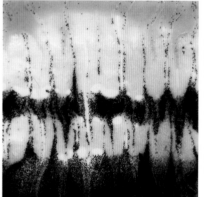
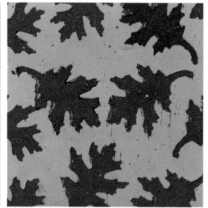

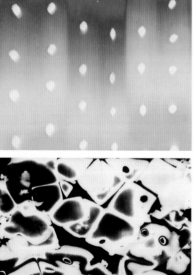

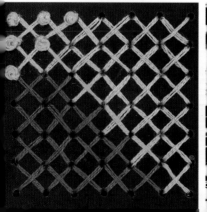

The Polymer Clay Artist's Guide

A directory of mixes, colors, textures, faux finishes and surface effects

Marie Segal

FIREFLY BOOKS

A FIREFLY BOOK

Published by Firefly Books Ltd. 2013

Copyright © 2013 Quarto Inc.

All rights reserved. No part of this publication
may be reproduced, stored in a retrieval system, or
transmitted in any form or by any means, electronic,
mechanical, photocopying, recording or otherwise,
without the prior written permission of the Publisher.

First printing

Publisher Cataloging-in-Publication Data (U.S.)
Segal, Marie.
   The polymer clay artist's guide : a directory of
mixes, colors, textures, faux finishes, and surface
effects / Marie Segal.
[160] p. : col. photos. ; cm.
Includes index.
Summary: Instructions to achieve a wide variety of
colors, textures, faux finishes, and surface effects with
polymer clay. Techniques are illustrated with practical
step-by-step photographs, and examples of finished
pieces of work from polymer clay artists.
ISBN-13: 978-1-77085-207-5
1. Polymer clay craft. I. Title.
731.42 dc23   TT297.S343   2013

**Library and Archives Canada Cataloguing
in Publication**
Segal, Marie
   The polymer clay artist's guide : a directory of
mixes, colors, textures, faux finishes, and surface
effects / Marie Segal.
Includes index.
ISBN 978-1-77085-207-5
1. Polymer clay craft--Handbooks, manuals, etc.
2. Polymer clay--Handbooks, manuals, etc. I. Title.
TT297.S44 2013   731.4'2   C2013-901208-7

Published in the United States by
Firefly Books (U.S.) Inc.
P.O. Box 1338, Ellicott Station
Buffalo, New York 14205

Published in Canada by
Firefly Books Ltd.
50 Staples Avenue, Unit 1
Richmond Hill, Ontario L4B 0A7

Conceived, designed and produced by
Quarto Publishing plc
The Old Brewery
6 Blundell Street
London N7 9BH

For Quarto Inc.:
Editor & designer: Michelle Pickering
Photographers: Marie Segal, Simon Pask
Picture researcher: Sarah Bell
Indexer: Dorothy Frame
Art director: Caroline Guest
Creative director: Moira Clinch
Publisher: Paul Carslake
QUA: PCJ

Color separation by Modern Age Repro House Ltd,
Hong Kong
Printed by 1010 Printing International Ltd, China

Publisher's note
Working with any craft materials and tools
requires common sense and due caution. Always
follow the manufacturer's advice on the package.
All statements, information and advice given in this
book are believed to be true and accurate. However,
neither the author, copyright holder nor publisher
can accept any legal liability for errors or omissions.

Contents

Introduction

Working with polymer clay should be fun and give you a feeling of accomplishment. The more skills you add to your body of knowledge, the more you will be able to achieve with your clay and your art.

The effects that you can create with polymer clay are many and varied. Polymer clay can be combined with a huge range of materials and adapted to many different applications. The more you play with the clay and try out different techniques, the more things that you will be able to achieve. This book is a compendium of easy-to-follow techniques and ideas to help you on your journey of exploration. Many of them are straightforward and easy to execute, so it does not matter how much experience you already have. Dip into the different sections of the book and simply try things out. Flip around to different pages and try combining the effects you find there. Such experiments will feed your creative mind and help you develop your own distinctive ideas and methods.

Although once marketed as a children's toy, polymer clay is now a fully fledged art medium in its own right. It combines beautifully with other mediums, opening up many avenues of experimentation. The techniques in this book can be applied to almost anything—jewelry, buttons, vessels, sculpture, home decorations and more—to add depth, dimension and beauty. Once you begin playing with polymer clay and trying out new techniques, you will soon find yourself able to create new effects and finishes of your own.

ABOUT THIS BOOK

The first chapter provides an overview of materials, tools and basic techniques for working with polymer clay. Use this information as a quick reference source whenever you need to brush up on the basics. The second chapter, the directory of effects, is what this book is really about. The effects are divided into seven general categories, and each category features three sections: techniques, tile samples and a gallery of finished pieces by polymer clay artists. The seven categories are designed to make the content of the book easy to access and digest, but don't treat each category as a separate entity. Combining techniques from different categories will open up far more opportunities for your polymer clay work.

Some words of advice

▪ Keep a journal to write ideas in. At first you may have ideas for effects that you cannot achieve because you have not yet learned the right technique. Keep a note of those ideas, draw what you think of and list words or thoughts to go with the images, then go forth, learn and play and someday you might be able to turn the piece in your mind into reality.

▪ If you cannot think of anything to make, use this book for stimulation. Open up the book to any page and try a technique that you find there. Open randomly to another page and try another technique, then combine them into something new.

▪ Even if you do not have the colors recommended on hand, do the project with a whole new color scheme—purple wood may become your new favorite!

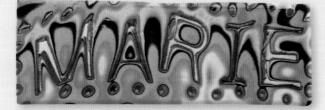

Techniques

Each category in the directory of effects starts with a selection of techniques. These demonstrate different methods of achieving a variety of effects, clearly explained with step-by-step photographs and instructions. The materials and tools required are listed, and there are also lots of tips as well as finished examples of poly-clay artwork made using the techniques.

Tile samples

After the techniques comes a selection of tile samples using a variety of materials and colors to showcase the effects that can be achieved with the techniques. The tiles are all the same size, making it easy to compare the different effects.

Polymer clay artists at work

At the end of each category you will find a gallery of finished examples of polymer clay artwork, with cross-references to tile samples made using the same or related techniques. Looking at the magic of polymer clay in the hands of such talented artists is one of the best forms of inspiration for anyone wishing to progress in this amazing craft.

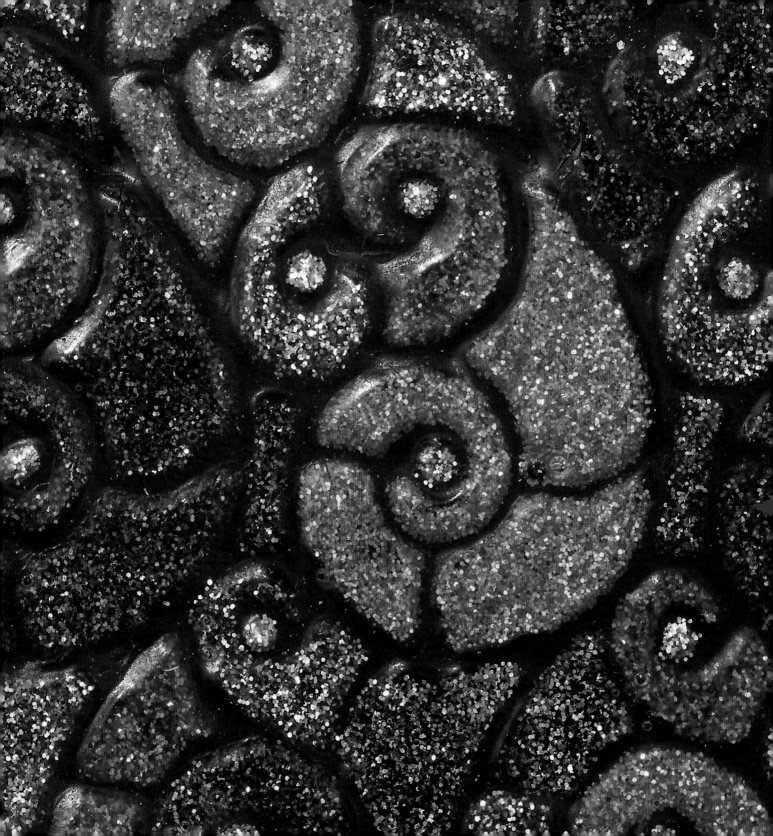

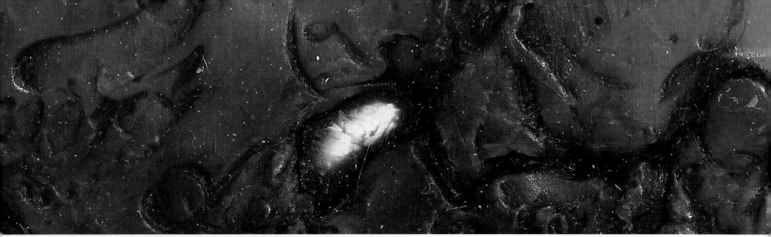

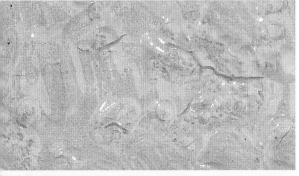

Getting started

TOOLS & MATERIALS

Materials

Oven-bake polymer clay is a mixture of PVC, resins, colorants, organic substances and plasticizers that are combined to form a clay-like substance that can be modeled, molded, sculpted, blended, textured and embellished. When the clay is baked, it becomes a solid plastic. Polymer clay combines beautifully with other materials and is perfect for mixed media work, making its creative potential virtually limitless.

Polymer clay

There are many types of polymer clay. Brands vary slightly in firmness and strength before and after baking, so test them to see which ones you prefer. The clay used in this book includes:

▪ **Colored clay:** Polymer clay is available in a huge range of opaque colors, and these can be mixed together to create an even larger color palette.

▪ **Metallic and special-effect colors:** Some metallic clays contain glitter for a sparkly effect, while others contain mica particles for creating mica shift and pearlescent effects. Special-effect clays include imitation stone and gem colors and fluorescent colors.

▪ **Translucent clay:** Translucent (or porcelain) clay is colorless. It can be used on its own or mixed with colored clay. Ready-mixed translucent colors are also available. Mixing translucent with metallic mica clays helps to spread out the mica particles to create more sparkle (mica clays on their own have a satin metallic finish). After baking, quench pieces containing translucent clay in ice water to enhance the translucency.

▪ **Liquid clay:** Liquid clay comes in all kinds of colors and in different clarities, some being more glass-like than others. Liquid clay can be used for gluing clay to clay, for softening standard clay and for simulating glazes. It can also be baked in molds, spread out to create sheets and used for image transfers—it is a versatile medium in its own right.

Vision du futur neck ornament

Anke Humpert

The colors of polymer clay are displayed beautifully in this 1¼in x 10ft (3cm x 3m) unisex neck ornament. It is made by covering wire armatures with polymer clay, and then the different-colored sections are riveted together.

Safety note

Polymer clay is nontoxic. It gives off a slight smell during baking, but this is not harmful. However, if you accidentally overheat the clay, it will burn. Burning plastic can give off fumes that may be toxic. If this happens, switch off the oven immediately (do not open it) and ventilate the room well. Leave the area until the fumes have cleared. Although polymer clay is nontoxic, it is not food-safe, so it should not be used for making vessels for eating or drinking.

Powders

■ **Mica powder:** Finely ground mica powders come in a huge range of colors, from metallics to iridescent colors. They can be mixed into raw clay or applied to the surface with a brush, fingertip or sponge. They can also be mixed into liquid clay, glaze, varnish or lacquer, and then painted onto baked clay and rebaked to heat-set the color. Brands include Jacquard Pearl Ex.

■ **Embossing powder:** This is made from resins and can be mixed into polymer clay and baked to create unusual imitative effects or simply to color the clay. It can also be applied to the surface of clay, where it will bloom to create a raised finish. The powder needs to be heat-set in an oven or with a heat gun. Don't touch until completely cool or the powder will smudge.

■ **Glitter:** Glitter can be mixed into clay, pressed onto the surface of raw clay or glued to baked clay. Good-quality glitter goes a long way and is inexpensive for the results you get. Test your glitters first on a small tile of polymer clay to see if it melts during baking or reacts unexpectedly. Brands include Art Institute Glitter and Martha Stewart Crafts glitters.

■ **Decorative chalk:** This can be applied in the same way as mica powder. Grate the stick of chalk on a coarse piece of sandpaper and store the grated powder in a jar. Beauty products like eye shadows (which have mica powders in them also) and blushes can be used as alternatives, as well as powdered unfired china glazes, kids' colored chalks and oil pastels.

Paints

■ **Acrylic paint:** This comes in both opaque and metallic colors. If you mix acrylic with a gel medium, you will get translucent paint. A water-based acrylic that dries on the surface of both raw and baked clay is the most useful type (some paints and inks never dry on raw clay). The advantage of this is that you can manipulate the clay after the paint has dried without marring the design. You can even run the clay through a pasta machine. To be sure of the paint adhering to the surface when applied to baked clay, put the piece back into the oven at 200°F (95°C) for 15 minutes. Allow to cool before touching. Brands include Jacquard acrylic fabric paints (Lumiere, Neopaque and Dye-na-Flow) and Golden acrylic paints.

■ **Oil paint:** Artists' oil paint is used to tint liquid polymer clay. It can also be applied in very thin washes to the surface of baked clay, but be aware that some oil paints can take a long time to dry.

Inks

■ **Alcohol ink:** These concentrated ink colors can be used to tint raw or baked polymer clay to create beautifully rich, jewel-like colors. Brands include Jacquard Piñata and Ranger Adirondack.

■ **Ink pads:** Working with stamps and ink pads is one of the most basic ways of printing onto polymer clay. Use solvent-based and metallic inks that dry completely on the surface of the raw clay so that you can continue to manipulate the clay after the ink has dried without smudging it. It is a good idea to mark the color name in bold black letters on the back of the ink pad so that you can tell at a glance what color it is. Brands include StazOn and Brilliance by Tsukineko and ColorBox Archival by Clearsnap.

■ **Pigment pens:** Permanent ink pens can be used to draw onto baked clay and add color. You can heat-set the inks in an oven or with a heat gun. Not all pens will work with polymer clay, so you need to test them first. Even though some pens say that they are permanent, they will bleed into the surface of the clay and look fuzzy over time. Brands include Rander Adirondack (fine-tipped) and Staedtler Lumocolor (thicker).

Metal leaf and foil

- **Metal leaf:** This comes in extremely thin sheets (almost skin-like) and in different colors. You can use real silver and gold leaf, but artificial metal leaf is far less costly and looks just as effective. It can be applied to the surface of raw clay and then baked. Apply a sealant to the finished piece to prevent the leaf from tarnishing. Suitable sealants include varnish, UV resin, a thin coat of liquid clay or a thin sheet of translucent clay. There is no need to use a sealant when the leaf is mixed into the clay.

- **Transfer foil:** These are thin sheets of polyester with color pigments attached to them. The sheets are laid onto the clay and pressure is applied to release the color, which can then be heat-set on the clay during baking. The color of some foils may change during baking, but the results are surprisingly durable and sealing is not essential. Brands include Kool Tak, Jones Tones and Lisa Pavelka.

Embellishments

A huge range of materials can be combined with polymer clay for decorative effect. They can be mixed into the clay as an inclusion, applied to the surface or embedded into the clay. Here are a few ideas:

- **Beads and gemstones:** You can attach any type of bead or stone to baked clay, but only use crystal or glass when applying to raw clay so that you can bake them in the oven along with the clay. Use a heat-set fabric glue that will cure at the same time as you bake the clay, or use hot-fix crystals that come with adhesive already on the back. Acrylic beads can be glued to baked clay.

- **Chains and charms:** These can be glued to the surface or embedded into the clay itself, or embedded in resin or encaustic wax. Try to avoid metal-plated plastic charms because they may change shape during baking. To tell if something is pure metal or has a plastic core, pop it in an oven at 275°F (135°C) for 30 minutes. Charms are also useful for making molds for embellishments.

- **Papers, fibers and fabrics:** Products designed for other crafts, such as cardmaking, scrapbooking and needlecrafts, often combine beautifully with polymer clay. JeJe peel-off stickers adhere well to clay, while Flower Soft, a type of ground-up paper, can be sprinkled onto clay for color and texture. Fabrics can be attached to the surface, threads can be cut up and mixed into the clay or the clay can even act as a canvas for embroidery.

Glue

Some glues just do not work with polymer clay and so you should always do a test when using a product for the first time.

- **PVA and fabric glue:** PVA provides an excellent, durable bond. Fabric glue can be baked with the clay and is then waterproof. Both can be used to glue materials such as fabric, beads and glitter to polymer clay. Brands include Crafter's Pick Ultimate glue and Art Institute Glitter's Dries Clear Fabric Adhesive.

- **Superglue:** This produces a permanent bond with polymer clay, even when applied quite thinly. It is good for gluing baked clay to baked clay, making it useful for repairs such as a broken leaf or a finger in a sculpture. Superglues are all similar but not all the same; most will become brittle if too hot or too cold. Brands include Gorilla Glue.

- **Epoxy glue:** This provides the strongest bond for gluing jewelry findings to clay. Wipe the findings with denatured alcohol to clean them and remove any grease before gluing.

Note: I would not recommend using hot glues with polymer clay. Regular white glues can be used but do not create a very strong bond.

Resin and finishes

▪ **Resin:** Clear resin is used to create enamel effects, and to embed and protect surface additions. It can be colored with oil paint. You can also create domed effects, adding a thin layer with embedded items and allowing it to cure, and then adding a domed layer on top. Two-part resin has to be mixed and left to cure; cover the piece to prevent dust from settling in the resin as it cures. UV resin takes the guesswork out of mixing and cures quickly in sunshine; you will need a UV lightbox when there is no sun. Brands include Lisa Pavelka Magic-Glos UV resin.

▪ **Varnish:** This is used as a sealant to protect surface finishes such as paints and powders, as well as for the look of the varnish itself. Varnishes come in matte, satin and gloss finishes. Water-based acrylic varnishes that look water clear are the ones you should use.

▪ **Gel medium:** This works in a similar way to liquid clay. It can be painted onto the surface of polymer clay to create glaze effects, mixed with inclusions and then painted onto the clay or used as a type of glue. Mix sand into the gel to make paint-on sand, for example, or use the gel to attach fabrics. Gel medium can be baked with the clay but does not need to be baked. Brands include Viva Decor Glass Effect Gel, Jacquard Neopaque Flowable Extender and Golden gel mediums.

Molding materials and solvents

▪ **Molding compound:** There are plenty of molds on the market, including silicone cake-decorating molds made for fondant, but you can also make your own. You can make rigid molds using polymer clay or flexible molds using two-part putty silicone molding compound. Brands include EasyMold by Environmental Technology.

▪ **Release agents:** When using polymer clay molds, you need to dust the mold with talcum powder, cornstarch, WD-40 or another type of oil or powder to help the clay release from the mold—the finer the release agent, the better. Some of the powder or oil will be left behind and may affect the look of the piece. This can be turned into an advantage by using mica powder as a release agent if you want the molded piece to have a pearlescent shimmer. Silicone molds only require a mist of water to prevent sticking.

▪ **Denatured alcohol:** Use this to degrease the surface of polymer clay before painting or gluing. It is also useful for cleaning up liquid clay and brushes that have been used with liquid clay; it also works fairly well for cleaning up encaustic wax. It is flammable, so dispose of rags and paper towels safely.

Tips & techniques

▪ Although polymer clay companies may tell you that their clays cannot be mixed with any of the other brands, many poly-clay artists do not find that to be the case. It is worth trying as many types of polymer clay as you can get your hands on. Mix them together, try out different techniques and bake the results.

▪ All sorts of materials can be combined with polymer clay to create a variety of different effects—there is only space to mention a few here. Some materials are designed specifically for use with polymer clay, but there are plenty more that can be used to create unique decorative effects. If you want to try a new product, make a test tile first before embarking on a large or important project.

▪ For efficiency, some artists prefer to carry out as many of the making stages as possible before baking. If you want to work this way, keep this in mind when choosing materials. Use a heat-set glue to attach rhinestones, for example, so that you can set the glue at the same time as baking the clay. You will still be able to add more elements after baking if you wish, but will only have to rebake for a short period of time.

▪ The choice of some materials is so vast that it can be confusing, so a few brand names have been included here. These have all been used to make the effects in this book and provided excellent results; more information can be found on page 160. This information is intended to help you, but not limit you. There are numerous other products available, and the only reliable way of discovering which product will create the result you want is to try it out for yourself.

TOOLS & MATERIALS

Tools

Your hands, a blade and an oven are about the only things you really need in order to start working with polymer clay. However, a few extra tools will allow you to achieve a wider range of effects and make your polymer clay work easier. See page 18 for information on baking equipment.

Work surface
You will need a smooth surface to work on, such as a marble or ceramic tile. Plastic cutting boards work nicely for traveling and are not so heavy.

Rolling tools
■ **Hand rolling tools:** Acrylic rollers and marble rolling pins are nonstick and perfect for rolling out sheets of clay. A clear acrylic roller allows you to see what is happening to the clay as you roll. You can use a ceramic tile or sheet of Plexiglas to help you roll smooth logs and canes. To roll clay to a specific thickness, place a rolling guide of that thickness on either side of the clay and roll across these. You can buy rolling guides or improvise with a pair of magazines, popsicle sticks, tongue depressors, pieces of wood or ceramic tiles. Bead rollers are available for rolling identically shaped beads.

■ **Pasta machine:** Although a pasta machine is not essential, you will soon find it invaluable when working with polymer clay. You can use it to condition the clay, roll out even sheets and mix colors and blends. Pasta machines come in different sizes and with different thickness settings, usually ranging from ⅛in (3mm) to less than 1/64in (0.5mm).

Cutting tools
■ **Blades:** A craft knife is useful for cutting clay from the block and cutting logs, but also for picking up and applying small pieces of clay. Very thin sheets of clay and liquid clay can be cut with scissors. Thin straight blades, called tissue, slicer or clay blades, are ideal for cutting straight edges and slicing canes. A steel scraper (from home-decorating stores) can be used instead of a tissue blade and is safer for children to work with. Ripple blades have a wavy cutting edge.

■ **Cutters:** Cutters come in numerous shapes and sizes for cutting out clay in different shapes. You can use cutters from confectionery and catering suppliers, as well as cutters designed for polymer clay. Some have plungers to push out the clay shape. Brands include Kemper Kutters' range of small brass cutters with plungers (designed for ceramic clay but great for polymer clay as well) and Makin's Clay Cutters.

Shaping tools

■ **Extruder:** An extruder is a barrel with a plunger at one end and a shaped die at the other. The barrel is loaded with clay and the plunger is pressed against the clay to push it out through the die. Different dies are used to make different shapes of extruded clay. The plunger mechanism may be operated by winding a handle, pressing with a thumb or squeezing a trigger.

■ **Molds:** Molds are an easy way to shape clay. There are plenty of molds on the market, including silicone cake-decorating molds made for fondant, as well as those designed specifically for polymer clay. You can also make your own using polymer clay or putty silicone.

■ **Modeling and sculpting tools:** There are several wonderful rubber-tipped tools for sculpting, including clay shapers and a wipe-out tool for smoothing. A wooden sculptor's thumb works well for large pieces and sculpts. Improvise with knitting needles, crochet hooks, dental tools, toothpicks and orange sticks. You can also make tools in polymer clay with different-shaped tips on the end.

Marking tools

■ **Rubber stamps and texture sheets:** You can use most rubber stamps with polymer clay. Some will need to be sprayed with a mist of water to help release the clay; clean the stamp if the clay starts to stick to it. Look for deeply etched stamps for impressing clay with textures and patterns, but the depth of the stamp is not important for printing onto clay. Most texture sheets require some form of release agent, such as a mist of water, and you cannot leave the clay on them for an extended period of time or it will be difficult to remove.

■ **Piercing tools:** Use a range of needles, from sharp sewing and darning needles to thick yarn needles, to pierce holes in beads and make marks in the clay. For easier handling, make your own needle tool by inserting the eye of the needle into a log of clay (like making a texture stick; see page 54). Alternatively, drill a hole in a small piece of wooden doweling and glue the needle into the hole. Other useful piercing tools include toothpicks, bamboo skewers and knitting needles. You can also drill holes through clay after baking; before baking, use a needle to mark a pilot hole to make drilling easier.

■ **Carving tools:** Carving tools and linoleum cutters are useful for carving patterns and textures into clay.

Improvised tools

Look around your own home and you will find lots of tools that you can use with polymer clay. Old kitchen equipment is usually a rich source: a garlic press for extruding clay strings for hair and squiggly patterns; a mini food processor for chopping clay and breaking it down faster for conditioning and mixing colors; a butter pat or egg slicer for marking lines and slicing canes; toothpicks for texturing clay, knitting needles for indenting holes and sewing markers for imitating lines of stitching. For hygiene reasons, once you have used a tool for polymer clay, you should not use it for food again.

BASIC TECHNIQUES

Working with polymer clay

The first thing you need to do when working with polymer clay is to condition it. This redistributes the PVC particles evenly throughout the clay to give it a more smooth and workable consistency. You can condition clay by kneading it in your hands for a few minutes, folding, rolling and twisting the clay until it becomes soft and malleable, but using a pasta machine is quicker and easier on the fingers.

> **You will need:**
> - Polymer clay
> - Pasta machine, roller and tissue blade
> - Round cutter and popsicle sticks (optional)
> - Baking tray, cardboard and baking parchment

Well-conditioned clay
Roll a ½in (13mm) thick log of clay and bend it in half. If it cracks, it needs more conditioning. If it bends, it is properly conditioned.

Conditioning the clay

- Start by warming the block of clay. You can put it (still in package) in your pants pocket or even sit on it, or use a heating pad on a low setting (no higher or you may bake the clay).
- Once the clay has warmed up, use a tissue blade to cut ⅛in (3mm) slices from the block. Roll one slice through a pasta machine on the thickest setting, then fold it in half, put the fold in the rollers and roll through again. Roll another slice in the same way, then put the two together and roll through the machine. Continue in this way, adding a new slice every once in a while.
- Another method is to use a small electric food chopper or processor; this adds a bit of heat at the same time. Cut a half block of clay into smaller pieces, put them into the machine and then pulse the "on" button in short bursts to break down the clay. Roll and press the chopped pieces of clay together by hand to form a pancake, then fold and roll through a pasta machine several times.
- Another option is to use a rubber mallet. Leave the clay in the package and hit it with the mallet until it starts moving. Then condition the clay by flattening it into a thin pancake and running it through a pasta machine or roll by hand.
- If you don't have a pasta machine, try rolling the clay with a heavy marble rolling pin to soften it, or use a "persuader" (a heavy steel rolling pin designed for conditioning clay and rolling canes).

Storing clay

- Until polymer clay is baked, it can be reused over and over. Store unused clay in a container such as a metal tin or polyethyline box to keep it free from dust. You can use #5 recycle plastic for storing clay, but beware that the placticizer in the clay will react with some types of plastic container. To counteract this, you can wrap the clay in baking parchment first. Wrapping is also useful for keeping sheets of clay and different colors separate, but do not use plastic wrap because this will react with the clay.
- Store the clay in a cool place away from heat and sunlight—polymer clay starts to bake at very low temperatures and can even start to cure if left on a window ledge. When buying clay, never leave it in your car on a sunny day. Bury it under a jacket if you have to leave it, or carry a small cooler with an ice pack if you know in advance that you will have to leave it.

Rolling balls, teardrops and logs

- To roll a ball, put a piece of clay into the palm of one hand, then cover it with your other palm. Rotate the top hand to shape the clay into a ball, gradually easing the pressure as the ball takes shape. If you need to roll several balls of exactly the same size, use a cutter of a suitable size to cut out disks of clay and roll those into balls.
- To turn a ball into a teardrop shape, press the edge of your upper hand onto one side of the ball and move your hand back and forth to form a point on that side. Alternatively, place the ball onto your work surface and use your fingers to roll one side of the ball into a point.
- To roll smooth, even logs, place the clay onto your work surface and roll it back and forth. Make the rolling movement long and fluid, rolling from the tips of the fingers to the base of the hand. Make sure that you roll forward and backward more than 360 degrees each time (short rolls with just the fingertips will produce bumpy logs). Don't press too hard. Let the surface you are using do the work; your hands are only guiding the clay.

Rolling sheets

- To roll by hand, place the roller on the center of the clay and then roll the clay as you would roll pastry. Lift the clay up from the work surface every now and again to loosen it so that it can lengthen. If you want the clay to stretch evenly in all directions, turn the sheet 90 degrees each time you loosen it from the work surface. When rolling very thin sheets, place the clay between two pieces of baking parchment as you roll so that you can lift it easily.
- Use rolling guides to roll a sheet to an exact thickness. Guides are available commercially or you can improvise. A pair of tongue depressors or even two magazine spines of the same thickness will do. Place the guides on either side of the clay and then roll over the top of the guides and the clay. Continue until the clay is reduced to the thickness of the guides.
- Rolling sheets with a pasta machine is quicker and easier. Feed the clay through the machine at the thickest setting—about ⅛in (3mm). Continue rolling the clay through the machine, reducing the thickness setting by one notch per roll, until the sheet is the required thickness.

Conditioning tips

- Some brands and colors of clay are firmer than others and require more conditioning. There is nothing wrong with the clay. Some clays are designed to be firmer for particular techniques, while for others it is just the personality of that particular product.

- Several companies make clay softeners that are designed to soften clay and make it easier to condition or to make older clay soft again.

- You can mix small amounts of mineral oil with polymer clay to make it a bit softer, but only use a very small amount and add it a little at a time so as not to overdo it. Another option is to put a small amount of petroleum jelly or hand lotion onto your hands and then mix it into the clay a little at a time. If conditioning the clay in a food processor, add a small amount to the bowl before chopping up the clay.

- Mixing a softer clay with a harder clay is another way to create a clay consistency that you like working with. You can also mix translucent clay with opaque colors to soften them.

- Another option is to roll out the clay as thinly as possible—about ⅛in (3mm)—with a marble or acrylic roller and then brush liquid clay onto the surface. Fold the clay sheet in half, place it in a suitable container or a Ziploc bag and leave it for a couple of days. Then take it out of the container and condition it, mixing in the liquid clay as you do so. You might prefer to wear gloves with this method.

- If the clay becomes very soft when you condition it, set it aside for a while before working with it so that it can cool and firm up a little. This will make the clay easier to shape and slice.

Making a tile sample

- Making a tile sample is a good way to try out materials and techniques. Make a tile of any new formulas and keep a note of what they are: the combination of clays, other materials and how the tile was made. A ½in (13mm) square or circle of clay is a handy size for gluing into a journal with your notes for quick reference.
- A 2in (5cm) square tile is the size used for demonstrating the techniques in this book. Make a cardboard template of your chosen size, lay it on top of the clay and use a tissue blade to cut the clay around the template. Clay with inclusions such as glitter can be hard to cut, so use the blade to mark the clay around the template. Remove the template and cut the clay along the marked lines, pressing hard to slice through the clay.
- When the embellishment on the front of the tile overhangs the edges, whenever possible turn the piece over and trim from the back because this is less likely to cause cracking. You can write the details about how the tile was made on the back.

Using clay as a veneer

- Using patterned clay as a veneer is an economical use of special mixtures and effects. To veneer a bead, for example, roll a ball of plain or scrap clay to form the core of the bead. To be really economical, apply small slivers and trimmings of decorated clay to the bead core. Stab the little pieces with the corner of your blade to pick them up and transfer them to the ball. It can look good if you leave spaces between the pieces for the color of the clay ball to show.
- To cover a bead completely with a veneer, use a round cutter of a suitable size to cut out a circle of the patterned clay to fit over half of the ball. Place the circle on the core bead like a cap, pulling the sides of the circle down on the ball of clay. Repeat for the other half of the ball, then roll the bead gently to smooth the joins.
- To make a hole for threading the bead, twist a wooden skewer into one side of the bead until the point of the skewer comes out the other side. Then twist the skewer out from the bead. Place the point of the skewer into the hole on the other side of the bead and twist into the same hole.

Baking polymer clay

- When polymer clay is baked, or cured, the PVC particles in the clay fuse together to form a solid plastic. Check the package for baking instructions because temperatures and timings vary between brands, but most recommend baking at 275°F (135°C) for about 30 minutes. Polymer clay can be rebaked multiple times, allowing you to build up complex projects in stages.
- Preheat the oven to the required temperature (buy an oven thermometer to double-check your oven's temperature settings because built-in thermostats are often inaccurate). Place the clay pieces onto a baking tray and bake for the required time. Allow the clay to cool (you can leave pieces in the oven to cool down or take them out) or quench in ice water.
- You can use your home oven to bake polymer clay. If you want to avoid the smell of the clay in your oven, bake your pieces inside a large roasting pan with a lid or cover with a tent of aluminum foil; dedicate the pan to your clay work. Place two ceramic tiles in the bottom of the pan with a layer of cardboard or cardstock on top, and rest your pieces on that. You may need to increase the baking time by about 10–15 minutes to heat up the pan. A pair of aluminum pans binder-clipped together with a layer of cardboard in the bottom also works well.

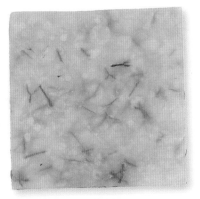

**Faux lampwork
Pandora-style beads**
Leila Bidler
These 1in (2.5cm) diameter beads with embedded spiral cane slices (made by rolling up strips of translucent and magenta clay with silver leaf sandwiched in between) are hand sanded and buffed, then coated with gloss varnish, to imitate the rich look of glass lampwork beads.

Quenching and plaquing

▪ Quenching involves taking baked clay hot out of the oven and plunging it into ice water. Always quench pieces made using translucent clay because it will maximize the translucency. Don't quench pieces that include glass, because the shock of the two temperatures may cause the glass to crack.

▪ Quenching can help to prevent clay from cracking because it causes the whole of the clay, both the outside and inside, to cool at about the same rate. It is worth quenching all larger pieces thicker than about ¾in (2cm). If something does crack, try healing the crack by returning the item to the oven, heating it back up to baking temperature for at least 15 minutes and then quenching the piece and leaving it to cool in the ice water.

▪ Plaquing refers to the little half-moon circles that can appear in the surface of the clay during baking. It is caused by trapped air or moisture. Adding any ingredient containing moisture will make the clay plaque more, and even sweaty hands may increase plaquing. Clay can pick up moisture from your hands during conditioning, so let the clay rest before working with it. Translucent and flesh clays and those without pigment are prone to plaquing (pigments disguise plaquing). Try mixing a ¼in (6mm) ball of opaque white into the 2oz (56g) pack of clay to mask the half moons.

Sanding and buffing

▪ Sanding and buffing can be used to give baked clay an attractive sheen and to maximize the transparency of translucent clays. Clays with inclusions can be sanded and buffed, but not items that have materials applied to the surface. Quenching makes sanding and buffing easier.

▪ You can sand polymer clay using sanding pads or wet and dry sandpaper. Pour a little water into a container and add a drop or two of dish soap or dishwashing liquid as a lubricant. Put the clay piece in the water and start sanding it, working systematically over the whole surface. Start with a coarse sandpaper (400 grit) and then gradually work through the grits to a fine sandpaper (2500 grit). The clay will feel smooth to the touch when you finish sanding with each grit; it will feel like you are not doing anything when it is time to change to a finer grit.

▪ After sanding, the clay will look dusty and needs to be buffed. You can rub the clay with quilt batting or a piece of cotton fabric, but using a mini drill or a bench grinder with a cotton buffing wheel is faster. Take care because the wheel can grab your piece and fling it out of your hand. A good rule is to hold tightly and buff lightly.

▪ A wax finish gives polymer clay a soft, warm glow. Apply the wax (such as Dorland's wax medium) to sanded clay, then use a soft cloth to buff the clay to a sheen. Waxing seems to intensify the colors after sanding.

Baking & finishing tips

▪ Baking on cardboard is a great idea to keep your trays clean. You can use cut-up cereal boxes to bake on, but make sure that you use the inside of the box with no print on it.

▪ It is safe to bake polymer clay in a home oven, but if you want to invest in an oven dedicated to your clay work, choose a good convection (fan-assisted) oven because this ensures that the heat is circulated more evenly throughout the oven. Avoid toaster ovens with exposed elements that will be too close to the clay, because this could lead to scorching or incomplete curing.

▪ Good-quality polymer clay does not have to be sealed for protection or to make it stronger, so as long as a piece has been well-made and baked correctly, there is no need to do anything further. The exception is if you have applied a surface finish such as metal leaf that needs to be sealed for protection. If this is the case, apply a coat of matte, satin or gloss varnish. You may also wish to varnish the clay simply because you want it to have a shinier finish (baked polymer clay has a matte finish). Alternatively, sand and buff it to give it a sheen.

BASIC TECHNIQUES

Color mixing

All brands of polymer clay come in a range of colors, and you can mix these to create new colors just like an artist mixes paint. You can mix by hand, but using a pasta machine is quicker. Mixing clays completely will create a uniform color, while partial mixing will produce a marbled effect. You can also create blends of two or more colors using the Skinner technique, which creates sheets of clay that blend smoothly from one color to another. When mixing a new color, start with a small test sample before mixing a larger quantity and keep a record of successful mixes.

You will need:

- Polymer clay in various colors plus translucent
- Pasta machine, roller and tissue blade
- Cardstock (the inside of a cereal box will do), scoring board, marker pen, large ball stylus and ruler

Mixing a color test sample
Roll out a log of each clay to the same thickness, then cut off the required number of equal-sized parts from each. Alternatively, roll sheets of the same thickness and use a cutter to cut out the number of parts required from each. Mix the parts together until they are a uniform color. Adjust the number of parts of each color as required.

Marbling
Roll logs of different colors and press together. Fold in half and roll again. Repeat this process as often as you like; the stripes of marbling will become finer the more you do it, but stop before the clay blends into a uniform color. Twisting the logs after each fold will produce random swirls of marbling.

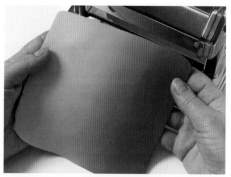

Skinner blend technique
1 Roll out sheets of clay in two different colors, ⅛in (3mm) thick. Cut a square of each color, just less than the width of the pasta machine. Use a tissue blade to cut across each square diagonally. Place two different-colored triangles together to form a square, fold in half and place the fold into the rollers of the machine.

2 Roll the folded clay through the machine on the thickest setting. Fold again, making sure that the side edges align, and roll again. Continue folding and rolling 10–15 times to achieve a smooth color blend. You can make blends of more than two colors using the same method.

If you make the diagonal cut about 1in (2.5cm) in from the corner, there will be an area of unmixed color at each side of the blend.

Use bar magnets to reduce the width of your pasta machine for making narrower blends.

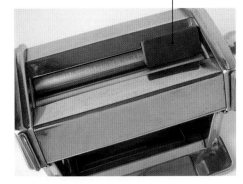

Use a marker pen to mark the center line on your scoring board so that it is easy to see.

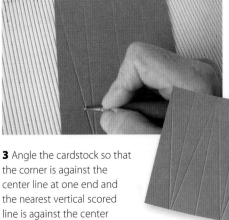

Skinner blend template

1 Templates are useful for making neat, accurate blends, and they also allow you to replicate blends precisely. Cut a strip of cardstock the width of the pasta machine and the length required. To make narrower blended sheets, place one or more bar magnets on the rollers of the machine to reduce the width and cut the cardstock to match that width.

2 Align the center of the cardstock with the center line on the scoring board and use a ball stylus to score along the center of the cardstock. Then find the center of each half of the cardstock to divide it into quarters (or divide it into the number of sections you require).

Cover magnets with clay or masking tape to stop them from scratching the pasta machine's rollers.

3 Angle the cardstock so that the corner is against the center line at one end and the nearest vertical scored line is against the center line at the other end. Use the ball stylus to score between the two points. Score the rest of the diagonal lines in the same way to divide the cardboard into triangles.

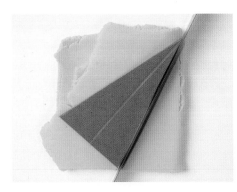

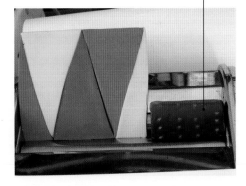

4 You will need to cut half triangles of clay for the edges of the blend and full triangles in between. Cut out a half and full triangle from the template, lay them onto the clay and cut around them. Alternatively, you can lay the uncut template over the clay sheets and run a finger up and down the diagonals; the scored lines will mark the clay below and you can cut along these marks.

5 Pass the clay through the pasta machine on the thickest setting (you may find it helpful to use a roller to roll and press the triangles together by hand before placing them in the machine rollers the first time). Fold in half, making sure that the side edges are aligned, and pass through the machine again. Repeat this process until you achieve a smooth blend.

Choosing colors

If you are intimidated by color, start with a few colors that you love—colors you like to wear or color combinations found in nature, for example. Paint chips from hardware stores are perfect little palettes for color inspiration. You can also use an artist's color wheel for guidance. Many clay companies provide color mixing charts on packaging and online, and there are classes about how to mix clay colors. There are also some brilliant websites; try searching for "color inspiration palettes." The palettes are often perfect for making blends. Bake a sample of each color mixture you make and glue it into a journal along with the formulation so that you have an exact record.

Color tints and shades

You can mix small amounts of colored clay into a base clay to create a range of tints and shades. This method is based on the Skinner technique (see page 20), and can be used to mix either separate colors or to create a smooth blend, depending on the placement of the colors within the base clay. The clay is rolled through the pasta machine on the thickest setting—about ⅛in (3mm)—unless stated otherwise.

The demonstration shows how to mix translucent colors, but the same technique can be used to create other tints and shades by replacing the translucent clay with another base clay. For example:

▪ Use pearl clay as the base to mix a range of pearlescent colors.

▪ Use gold or silver clay as the base for metallic colors. Gold gives the subtle but rich look of old tapestries, while silver produces a cool, shimmery effect reminiscent of dichroic glass.

▪ A base of white clay will produce bright but sherbet-like pastel colors, while a gray base clay will create smoky colors.

▪ A base of champagne clay will produce a Victorian color palette, with hints of the tea-stain look of antique pieces.

▪ Use flesh clay as the base for muted, toned-down colors.

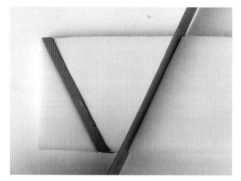

Mixing translucent colors

1 Roll out the translucent clay (or other base clay; see box, left) and fold in half to double the thickness. Trim the folded sheet to fit the width of your pasta machine; the height can vary, depending on how much clay you wish to mix. The folded sheets used here are 1¼ x 4in (3 x 10cm). Cut a small triangle off one end. Roll out some colored clay and cut a ¼in (6mm) wide strip. Alternatively, place the cut edge of the translucent triangle onto the colored clay and cut around it. Another option is to roll out a log of colored clay, flatten it and then cut off a strip.

2 Press the triangle and colored strip back onto the edge of the main translucent sheet so that everything sticks together. Trim the ends of the colored strip to fit if necessary. Make another cut through the translucent sheet (see below for guidance on where to make the cut) and add the next strip of color. Continue adding colored strips until you reach the end of the translucent sheet, arranging the strips as shown below. Roll the completed sheet with a roller to tack all of the pieces together.

Leave a gap of about ¼in (6mm) between colored strips.

Strip arrangement for separate colors

You can add a short color strip at the end if there is not enough room for a full strip—the idea is to mix as many colors as possible, as quickly as possible.

Cross the colored strips by about ¼in (6mm).

Strip arrangement for blended colors

Trim the end if necessary so that the whole thing will fit through the opening on the pasta machine.

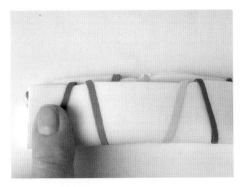

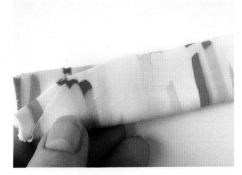

3 Pass the sheet through the pasta machine, then fold it in half, making sure that the side edges are aligned (this is more important than aligning the top and bottom edges). Press along the fold, then place the fold into the opening of the pasta machine and roll through. Continue folding and rolling in this way.

4 You will soon begin to see the colors mixing into the translucent clay. Take care that you always align the side edges. This is important when mixing colors that you wish to keep separate (if you cross colors, they will blend together), but also for achieving a smooth transition between colors that you do want to blend them together.

5 If the top and bottom edges become very out of shape, flip the folded sheet from left to right to even it out a little. You will need to fold and roll the sheet through the machine about 20–25 times in total.

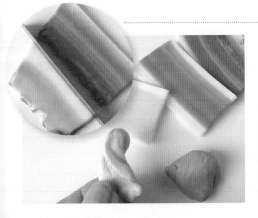

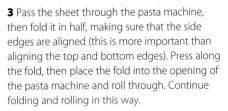

Separate colors
When the sheet is mostly mixed, you should have different colors divided by narrow strips of plain translucent. Cut across the translucent areas to separate the colors. Mix each section by hand until it is a uniform color. You will now have several translucent colors without having to mix each one individually.

Blended colors
Continue folding and rolling the sheet through the pasta machine until the colors are blended as you require. It should eventually become a continuous blend from one edge of the sheet to the other.

Long strip
To make a long strip of clay such as for spiral canes (see page 80), fold the blended sheet in half as before, but this time pass it through the pasta machine on its side edge. Then pass it through again on the ³⁄₃₂in (2mm) setting. You can do the same thing with the sheet used for separate colors if you want a long strip of that mixture.

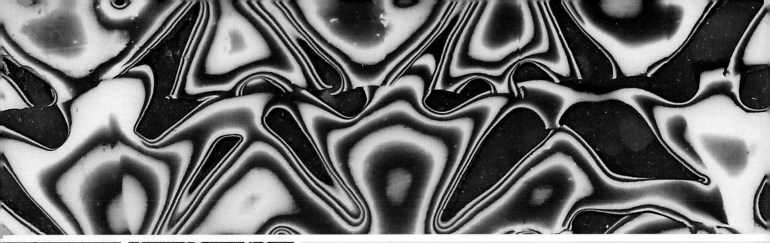

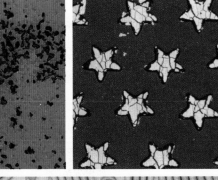

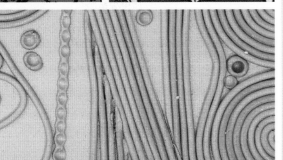

Directory
of effects

INCLUSIONS & ADDITIONS

Mixing inclusions into clay

Inclusions, or mix-ins, are materials that are mixed into raw polymer clay to create interesting color, pattern and textural effects. Anything that can withstand baking can be mixed into the clay, including glitters, dried flowers and herbs, mica and embossing powders, fibers, baked polymer clay and even foil candy wrappers. Any type of clay can be used, but translucent clay is especially effective because the inclusions will be visible within the body of the clay.

You will need:

- Pasta machine, roller and tissue blade
- For candy wrapper sample:
  » Translucent clay
  » Pure-foil candy wrappers (paper-lined foil is unsuitable unless you can peel off the paper)
  » Scissors
- For baked clay sample:
  » Brown and dough-colored clay (such as Cernit champagne clay)
  » Stiff brush or sandpaper
  » Soft brush and caramel-colored decorative chalk or matte make-up (such as eye shadow)
  » Matte varnish
- For rose and glitter sample (overleaf):
  » Translucent clay
  » Dried rose petals
  » Glitter: powder and slivers

Candy wrapper foil

1 Inclusions such as foil and embroidery threads need to be cut up before you can mix them into the clay—⅛in (3mm) pieces work well. Smooth out the foil and cut into ⅛in (3mm) wide strips, leaving one edge uncut to keep the strips joined together for ease of handling. Cut across the strips to make lots of small pieces.

2 Roll out the clay, ⅛in (3mm) thick. Press the clay sheet onto the cut pieces of foil, gathering up all the little sections with the clay. Check to see if there are any bare spaces on the clay and then press those areas onto the foil until the clay is evenly covered.

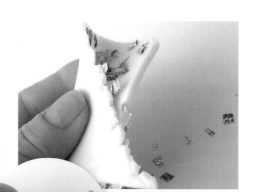

3 Fold the clay in half with the foil on the inside. If pieces of foil fall out, press the folded clay onto them to pick them up.

4 Roll out the clay, then fold in half and roll again. Continue until the foil pieces are distributed evenly through the clay. Bake and quench, then sand and buff to maximize translucency—the foil will show through the clay to produce a very rich, unique look. Although silver and gold wrappers are used here, try using foil in other colors and patterns—it's a great way to recycle and, perhaps best of all, you get to eat chocolate for your art!

Baked clay

1 Roll out the brown clay, ⅛in (3mm) thick, and fold in half to double the thickness. Use a tissue blade to cut the clay sheet into ¼in (6mm) wide strips, then cut the strips into roughly ¼in (6mm) pieces to simulate chocolate chunks. Bake and allow to cool.

2 Roll out the dough-colored clay, ⅛in (3mm) thick. Place the cooled chocolate chunks in the center of the sheet (if they are too hot, they will start to cure the raw clay). Fold up the sheet around the chunks. Press the clay together and mix as best you can by hand until the chunks are evenly dispersed (this mixture will not go through a pasta machine).

3 Form the clay into the best ball that you can make with the hard chunks in it. Flatten the ball with your palm to form a cookie shape. Firmly press a stiff brush or some sandpaper into the top surface of the cookie. Press hard onto the chocolate pieces to push back the cookie clay and expose some of the chunks.

4 Using a soft brush, apply caramel-colored chalk or matte make-up, starting around the bottom edge of the cookie. Apply the color a little lighter as you move up the cookie. Bake and allow to cool, then apply a coat of matte varnish to stop the powder from rubbing off.

Chocolate chip cookie

Mixing baked clay chocolate chunks into the cookie rather than simply applying them to the surface produces a more realistic result. The finished cookie would make a great fridge magnet.

Saving clay scraps

Everything in polymer clay can be used for something. Save scraps of baked clay from drilling and carving for use as inclusions (see tile 17, page 39). You may find it useful to keep similar colors together when storing the scraps.

Summer sorbet bracelet
Bea Grob
Different colors of glitter and mica powder are mixed into translucent clay. The clay is pressed into little patties with textures on both sides, baked and then strung on elastic cording alternated with seed beads.

Rose petals and glitter
1 Use this method for mixing in any type of dried herb, glitter, powder or small particles. Roll out the clay, ⅛in (3mm) thick. You will be folding the clay sheet roughly into thirds when mixing in each material. Place a single layer of dried petals in the center third of the sheet, then fold one of the outer thirds of the clay sheet over the petals.

2 Fold over the remaining third of the sheet, then pinch the top and bottom ends of the folded clay together to trap the petals inside. Squeeze the clay together, twisting and rolling it to mix the petals into the clay. The petals will break up if they have been dried completely. If any pieces of petal fall out, pick them up by pressing the clay onto them and then continue mixing.

Drying fresh rose petals
Old rose petals smell heavenly when mixed into polymer clay. The petals need to be completely dried so that they break up well during mixing, maintain their color and do not decay. To dry fresh petals, stack two paper towels on top of each other and fold in half. Place the petals between the folded layers (the paper towels will absorb the moisture from the petals), then put everything inside a heavy book. Stack more books on top and set aside until dry. The drying time will depend on the humidity in your area, and can take up to a couple of weeks.

3 Roll out the petal clay mixture, ⅛in (3mm) thick. Sprinkle some powdered glitter over the center third of the clay sheet. Keep the glitter away from the top and bottom edges by about ¼in (6mm). Spread the glitter into a thin layer. If the glitter is too thick, it will fall out of the clay while you are mixing; if you want to add a lot of glitter, it is better to add it in two or more stages.

4 Fold the sheet into thirds again, trapping the glitter inside. Pinch the open ends closed. Mix by hand as before, or run through a pasta machine on the thickest setting, then fold the sheet in half and roll through the machine again, placing the fold into the rollers first. Continue in this way, folding and rolling until the glitter is dispersed evenly throughout the clay.

5 Next add some slivers of glitter to the clay. These are a little hard to scoop out with a spoon, so add a pinch at a time. Spread the slivers out flat on the center third of the clay, fold the clay to trap the glitter slivers inside and then mix together thoroughly as before. Mix in a second layer of slivers if required.

6 You can see the translucency of the clay here when it is rolled very thinly. After baking, maximize the translucency by taking the clay hot out of the oven and quenching it in ice water. Sanding and buffing will also enhance translucency. When using dried petals and herbs, do not keep the baked clay immersed in water for too long because any herbs that are not completely encapsulated within the clay may absorb the water and swell. You may wish to seal your pieces with a coat of varnish or resin for better resistance to humidity.

Trinity necklace
Michele Norine
The large focal bead is composed of three polymer clay faux granite and patterned cabochons. The faux granite is made from raw translucent clay mixed with scraps of baked clay; the scraps were collected when drilling holes through other beads and then loosely sorted into color groups. After baking, the cabochons are sanded and buffed and then assembled into a textured clay bezel with silver highlighted accents. The polymer clay focal bead is strung with genuine lapis lazuli chips, amber agate beads and oxidized sterling silver beads.

Tips & techniques

- Mixing inclusions into clay can be messy, so work over a piece of paper or cardboard. Cardboard shoeboxes are ideal—store everything in the box and work over the lid to catch spillages.

- Plastic ice-cream tasting spoons are handy for scooping and spreading glitter, sand and powders onto clay.

- Avoid fresh ingredients that might decay. Petals, leaves, herbs and citrus peel can be used as mix-ins, but they need to be thoroughly dried first or they will turn brown when baked and will gradually decay. Any moisture will also increase plaquing during baking.

- Organic materials will retain their smell for some time after baking, so keep this in mind when combining different ingredients. Woody herbs retain their fragrance longer than delicate herbs and flowers. Adding a small amount of essential oil will fragrance the clay for a while, but may increase plaquing in translucent clay.

- Avoid mixing salt or sugar into clay because these hygroscopic materials will gather moisture and weep after a while, making the clay feel sticky.

- Be aware that some materials, such as glitter slivers, can make the clay a little harder to cut.

- Be careful of rolling clay containing hard inclusion materials through a pasta machine because this could damage the rollers of the machine. It might be a good idea to use a cheaper or older machine for inclusion work, or to mix by hand instead.

- Always protect baking trays with cardstock or cardboard when baking clay containing inclusions. This will also help to avoid transferring mix-ins to another piece being baked.

INCLUSIONS & ADDITIONS

Paints and powders

The surface of polymer clay can be decorated with all sorts of paints and powders. These materials can be brushed, sponged, rubbed, sprinkled, glued or pressed onto the clay. Powders will adhere to the tacky surface of raw clay, while paints can be applied before or after baking. You can mask off areas of clay to keep them free from color, or use stencils to apply patterns and motifs. Protect surface decorations with a sealant such as lacquer or varnish.

You will need:

- Polymer clay pieces to be decorated

- Glitter in various colors, glitter glue with fine nozzle and old toothbrush

- Acrylic paints, mica powders, ink pads and fabric paint (such as Lumiere 3D)

- Stencil brush and sponge applicator

- Masking material, such as sequin scrap, and punched paper stencils

- Cardstock and old towel

- Liquid clay, oil paints, mixing palette, toothpick, mineral oil, fine paintbrush and denatured alcohol

Parrot pendant

Marie Segal

Glitter is perfect for decorating a tropical parrot pendant. The parrot is designed so that there are defined sections for applying the glitter. Cutters are used to indent markings on the leaves; the wings, body and tail of the parrot are built from separate clay logs; and additional markings are made with a ball stylus or knitting needle.

Glitter

1 Glitter can be pressed onto the surface of raw clay, but you will need to use glue to apply glitter to baked clay. Work over a sheet of paper to catch spillages. Using a fine nozzle on the glue bottle, apply a little glue to the first area you want to cover—here, the sections of a leaf between the marked veins. Apply just enough glue so that it domes slightly but without running.

2 Scoop out some glitter and sprinkle it over the glued section, making sure that all of the glue is covered. Wait 10–20 seconds to allow the glitter to settle into the glue, then shake off the excess. Tap the clay piece onto the edge of the jar to knock off as much excess glitter as possible. Cover the remaining leaves in the same way (or all the areas using this color). Pick up the paper and pour any spilled glitter back into the jar.

3 Apply glitter to other areas of the design as required, completing one color at a time. When complete, let the piece dry for 24 hours. Use an old toothbrush to scrub off any excess glitter that is not stuck to the clay, then rebake the piece to heat-set the glue.

Pearlescent flower brooch

Marie Segal

Mica powders mixed with acrylic lacquer add rich, shimmering color to this flower brooch. The lacquer gives the color mixture a dimensional quality.

Shake the jar of mica powder and then use whatever powder is stuck inside the lid.

Highlighting

Mica powders, available in metallic, pearlescent and iridescent colors, are great for highlighting textured designs. Rub a fingertip into the powder in a circular motion to spread out any clumps of powder, then brush your fingertip lightly over the clay (don't press on the raw clay). Chalks and waxes can be rubbed on in the same way.

Masking

Lightly press the masking material onto the clay. Press the corner of a piece of foam sponge into some mica powder; tap the sponge a couple of times to shake off any lumps. Lightly press the sponge onto the masked clay. Don't rub it across the clay; lift it and then press down onto new areas. When complete, carefully lift off the mask.

Stenciling

1 Lightly press the stencil onto the clay. Dip a stencil brush into some acrylic paint and then wipe off the excess. Dab the brush onto the stencil design, using an up-and-down motion to avoid paint bleeding into other areas. It is almost impossible to reposition a stencil exactly, so check carefully that all spaces are covered.

2 Carefully peel the stencil off the clay and let the paint dry. You can create interesting effects by overlapping areas of stenciling. Place another stencil overlapping the dried paint and use an ink pad to pat ink onto the clay. The stenciled paint will show through the ink, but the ink will change the color of the paint.

3 Continue stenciling designs onto the clay. Here, a make-up sponge is being used to apply mica powder through the stencil. Don't press too hard; you just want to deliver the powder to the surface of the clay evenly, not texture the clay or press it out of shape. Blow off any excess powder over a trash can or outside.

Antiqued queen of hearts brooch

Marie Segal

This highly textured piece, with molded motifs on a fleur de lis pavé background, is antiqued with a wash of brown acrylic paint. The paint is rubbed off the raised areas to leave color in the crevices to simulate the aged look of an antique piece.

Work with baked clay so that you can press paint into all the recesses and textured areas without spoiling the design.

Staining and antiquing

1 Dip a stencil brush into some acrylic paint and then wipe off the excess. If using a paste-like paint, dab the brush up and down in the jar lid or on some cardstock to make sure that the brush is not overloaded. Holding the brush vertically, dab it up and down onto the clay, punching the color into the recesses of the design.

2 When the clay is completely covered, lift it up and check that all of the edges are painted as well. On the left next to my thumb, you can see that there is no paint under the edge of one of the leaves; punch more paint into this area.

3 Let the paint sit for a little until it looks matte rather than shiny (this may only take a couple of minutes in hot weather). Dampen an old towel and use it to wipe off the paint from the raised areas of clay. Use the towel to scrub off the paint if it has dried too much. If the paint is still too wet and comes off too easily, you can repeat the staining process in that area.

4 Any recesses or deep texture marks in the clay will retain the paint. Keep this in mind when texturing or incising patterns into your clay pieces. The deeper the impression, the easier it is to stain without wiping off too much paint. The more porous the surface, the shorter time you have before wiping off the excess. The smoother or denser the clay surface, the longer you can leave the paint before wiping.

5 To add metallic highlights, place a small drop of metallic acrylic paint onto some cardstock. Rub a finger in the paint and then apply over the surface of the clay, a little at a time, to add shimmer to the raised areas of the design. You can apply several colors, allowing them to blend where they overlap.

Liquid clay glazing

1 Use liquid clay to apply a colored glaze to your pieces. Mix the colors you require in a mixing palette. Add 1 tsp (5ml) of liquid clay to each well and use a toothpick to stir in a small amount of oil paint. Add a couple of drops of mineral oil to thin the mixture to a glaze-like consistency so that it will go onto the clay smoothly.

2 Paint the different colors onto the clay design to give the impression of glazing. You can apply a liquid clay glaze to baked or raw clay, but in the latter case take care to use a light hand and a soft brush unless you want to texture the clay as well. Clean brushes with denatured alcohol between colors. Bake the finished design to cure the liquid clay glaze.

Fabric paint

1 Fabric paint is designed for application to a flexible surface, so many fabric paints work beautifully on polymer clay. The paint being used here is dimensional and also works as a glue, making it perfect for attaching rhinestones, charms and so on. A baked clay tile is being decorated here. Allow the paint to dry completely; it can also be baked on the clay.

2 Use the finest—¹⁄₆₄in (0.5mm)—nozzle on the bottle of paint for drawing design details. Here, a rubber stamp and permanent ink have been used to print an image onto a clay tile and then baked. Lines of paint are then drawn over some of the lines of the image as embellishment. Let the paint dry completely, rebaking if you wish.

Tips & techniques

▪ To keep your clay area free from glitter and powders, it is a good idea to apply these materials in a different work area. Work over scrap paper or a shoebox lid to catch spillages.

▪ Both surface decoration and clay will change color slightly during baking, so make test pieces to check colors.

▪ An old towel that has become a bit rough is ideal for rubbing off acrylic paint when staining or antiquing. If you let the paint dry too much, you can use the rough fabric to scrub off the paint. You can also add a little soap to the towel if you need to remove paint after a few days (if you have changed your mind or simply forgotten).

▪ Liquid clay gives the impression of ceramic glazes on some colors of polymer clay (such as champagne and terracotta-colored clay) more than others. The liquid clay paint is durable and will become part of the clay piece after it is baked. It can also be used as a glaze with no color added. When you mix oil paint with liquid clay, it will be somewhat translucent after baking. You can make the glaze more opaque by adding a very small amount of white oil paint as well as the color.

▪ You can mix other materials into liquid clay instead of oil paint. Try adding stone-like embossing powders to make paints for simulating stone effects. Mix in some white embossing powder or white sand to create brush-on "snow." Add a small amount of white or crystal glitter to make the snow sparkle.

▪ Embossing powders will bloom on the clay surface and, if touched when warm, can be smeared or the effect marred by your fingers. Do not handle until completely cool after baking.

INCLUSIONS & ADDITIONS

Metal leaf, foil and alcohol ink

The intense colors of alcohol ink are perfect for tinting clay, especially translucent and lighter clays. When combined with metal leaf or foil, the result is rich and jewel-like. Just a drop or two of ink added to translucent clay will replicate shimmering frosted glass, while stronger colors are perfect for simulating semiprecious stones and enamel. Exposed metal leaf will tarnish, so apply a sealant such as varnish or resin.

You will need:

- Pasta machine or roller
- Transfer foil and tissue blade
- For faux enamel:
  » White or black polymer clay
  » Silver metal leaf and soft brush
  » Rubber stamp or texture sheet
  » Alcohol inks in several colors
  » UV resin
- For lapis lazuli:
  » Translucent clay with tiny amount of white mixed in
  » Gold metal leaf
  » Sapphire blue alcohol ink

Metal leaf

1 Roll out a sheet of clay. Open the packet of metal leaf and remove the protective tissue paper, leaving the leaf in the packet. Metal leaf blows around and sticks to things very easily, so never work in a breezy area. Carefully lay the clay on top of the leaf and press down gently. Use a tissue blade to trim the leaf around the clay (metal leaf does not cut very well).

2 Lift the clay sheet and turn it over; the cut metal leaf will have stuck to the clay. Use a soft brush to smooth the leaf over the surface and around the edges; take extra care with this stage if the leaf is to remain on the surface rather than being mixed in. Use the brush to apply small pieces of leaf if there are gaps.

Transfer foil

1 Lay the foil, colored side up, over a sheet of clay (the reverse of the foil is usually dull gold or silver). Rub across the surface with your fingers to stick the foil in place and warm it up.

2 Scrape a tissue blade across the surface of the foil; some scratches will appear if you are doing it correctly. Scrape across in all directions—top to bottom, left to right and so on. Take hold of an edge of the foil sheet and rip it swiftly off in a single motion. The foil should remain on the clay.

Inlaid veneer rings

Meredith S. Arnold

Up to 20 layers of liquid clay are built up, with different mediums—including metal foils, fabric paints and fibers—applied to each layer and baked before the next layer is added. The layered sheet is then cut into shape, inserted into the rings and covered with resin.

Enamel pendant
Marie Segal

Polymer clay faux enamel is embellished with applied metal shapes and charms in a bed of glossy UV resin.

Faux enamel

1 Apply silver leaf to a sheet of clay and then impress with a rubber stamp; the leaf will prevent the stamp from sticking. Add small drops of alcohol ink, holding the ink bottle horizontally to get a slow, steady flow of ink. You can blow on the wet ink to spread it (protect your work surface with paper or cardboard when doing this).

2 Add highlights to the design with a few drops of white ink, taking care not to distort or mark the design. You can also apply the ink with a cotton swab, as well as use a swab with clean-up solution to take off excess ink. Allow the ink to dry, then bake. Once the clay has cooled, apply a coat of resin for a hard enamel finish.

Lapis lazuli

1 Spread blue alcohol ink onto a sheet of translucent clay. Let the ink dry slightly until it looks matte rather than shiny; it will then make less mess when mixing it into the clay. Fold the sheet in half, with the ink on the inside, then twist and roll the clay to mix in the ink (you may wish to wear gloves to do this).

2 Roll out the blue mixture and apply a sheet of gold leaf. Fold the clay in half with the leaf on the inside, then mix thoroughly by hand so that the leaf breaks up into small pieces.

3 Twist, roll and flatten out the clay until the leaf looks evenly distributed. The finished mixture will look a lot darker, and more like lapis lazuli, after it has been baked. Quench the baked clay in ice water to increase the translucency and enhance the look of semiprecious stone. Omitting the metal leaf will give the look of frosted sea glass.

Marbled cabochon
Alcohol ink partially mixed into translucent clay will produce an attractive marbling effect.

INCLUSIONS & ADDITIONS

Tile samples

Polymer clay can be combined with all sorts of different mediums and additives, either mixed into the clay, applied to the surface or a combination of both. There are all kinds of substances to choose from, including glitters and embossing powders for dazzling variations; metal leaf, foils, paints and inks for imitative replicas; herbs and organic materials for unusual effects; metallic and opaque paints for antiquing; and powders and chalks for accenting—the list is virtually endless. All of the tile samples featuring inclusions mixed into the clay are made using ¼–½ tsp (1–2.5ml) of the mix-in per 1in (2.5cm) ball of clay. The exact quantity you use will depend on the look you wish to achieve, so have fun experimenting.

Rock'n horse brooch
Judy Summer
The mane and tail are sculpted from black clay and attached to a wire armature. Different colors of embossing powder are mixed with separate batches of translucent clay, then small balls of the mixtures are added to the armature to complete the horse.

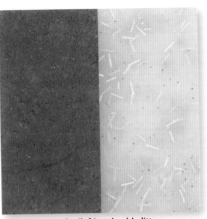

Red glitter powder (left) and gold glitter slivers (right).

GLITTER

1 Sparkler
Red glitter powder and gold slivers; translucent clay
How-to: Roll out clay and sprinkle with glitter. Fold the clay to trap the glitter inside and mix (see page 28). Add more glitter, a little at a time, until you like the way it looks.

2 Bling bling
Red glitter; red clay
How-to: Sprinkle thin layer of glitter onto a paper plate and press rolled out sheet of clay onto the glitter. Check to see if any areas of clay are bare and press those areas into glitter again. Roll the back of the clay with a roller to press the glitter into the clay. Using the same color clay and glitter gives a rich, vibrant result, but you can try other combinations as well.

3 Glitter flower
Glitter in various colors and glitter glue; black clay
How-to: Apply clay petal and leaf shapes to a background tile and then bake (see page 140). When cool, apply glue to the areas you want to decorate with the same color glitter. Sprinkle the glitter over the glue, allow to settle and then shake off the excess (see page 30). Repeat for each area of color.

4 Glitter cloisonné

Glitter in various colors, glitter glue and UV resin; black clay

How-to: Roll out a thick sheet of black clay, impress deeply with a rubber stamp and then bake. Working with one glitter color at a time, fill the deep spaces with glue and then apply glitter (see page 30). Complete the look of cloisonné by covering with resin.

7 Crystal glass

Viva Decor clear glass-effect gel; gold clay

How-to: Apply gel to surface of raw clay, swirling it around to create texture. Allow to dry, then bake. The gel dries transparent to give a three-dimensional glossy finish. It is available in several colors as well as clear. For a smooth glossy surface, apply a bead of gel across one edge of the clay and use an old credit card or similar tool to spread the gel.

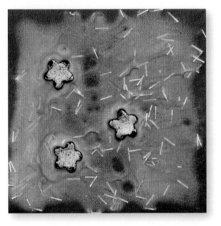

5 Midnight stars

Gold leaf, glitter slivers, mica powder and liquid clay; black and blue clay

How-to: Apply gold leaf to black clay (see page 34). Use a cutter to cut out small stars and then bake. Baking will make the stars easier to handle; you can pick them up with tweezers. Mix mica powder into liquid clay and paint the mixture onto a sheet of blue clay. Sprinkle with glitter slivers, add some gold stars and then bake.

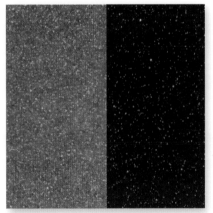

Verdigris embossing powder mixed into translucent clay (left) and black clay (right).

EMBOSSING POWDER

8 Verdigris shimmer

Verdigris embossing powder; translucent and black clay

How-to: Roll out clay and sprinkle with verdigris embossing powder. Fold the clay to trap the powder inside and mix (see page 28). Keep adding powder until you achieve the effect you require.

SPRINKLES & GEL

6 Color explosion

Paper Soft paper sprinkles and UV resin; red clay

How-to: Apply resin to surface of baked clay, drop paper sprinkles into the resin and allow to cure. Designed for cardmaking and scrapbooking, paper sprinkles are also perfect for adding color and texture to polymer clay.

9 Patinated copper

Verdigris embossing powder; translucent clay

How-to: Sprinkle thin layer of verdigris embossing powder onto a paper plate. Gently press a sheet of clay onto the powder. A slightly uneven application of powder will enhance the effect of patinated copper.

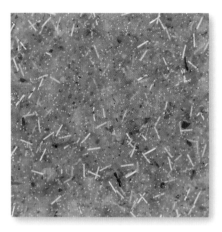

ORGANIC INCLUSIONS

10 Rose paper
Dried rose petals and glitter powder and slivers; translucent clay
How-to: Roll out the clay, add a layer of dried rose petals and mix in (see page 28). The roses will break into small pieces and the clay will look like handmade paper with roses in it. Add glitter powder and sprinkles in the same way.

Jade rose bead with dragonfly
Marie Segal
The sage and translucent mixture from tile 13 is used to sculpt a rose, with each petal shaped and added one at a time. A small molded dragonfly in gold clay is applied to one of the petals. The bead is stained with brown acrylic, as tile 13, and then highlights of gold mica powder are brushed on.

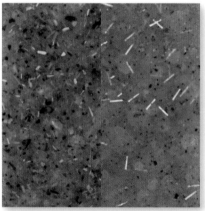

11 Wake up and smell...
Chamomile tea, black pepper and glitter slivers; translucent clay
How-to: Roll out clay and sprinkle with your chosen inclusion. Fold the clay to trap the material inside and mix (see page 28). The clay will retain the scent of teas and spices. Caution: Pepper may cause sneezing when mixing!

Chamomile tea (left) and black pepper with glitter slivers (right).

13 Old jade
Dried sage and brown acrylic paint; translucent clay mixed with tiny amount of white clay
How-to: Roll out clay and sprinkle with dried sage. Fold the clay to trap the herb inside and mix (see page 28). Roll out clay again, apply a wash of brown acrylic, then wipe off the excess to achieve the antique look of old stone (see page 32).

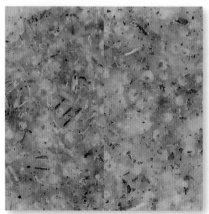

12 Fresh and fragrant
Dried lavender and peppermint leaves; translucent clay
How-to: Roll out clay, sprinkle with dried lavender or peppermint, fold the clay to trap the material inside and then mix (see page 28). If using fresh lavender or peppermint, dry the ingredients thoroughly before mixing them into the clay. Crush or grind the peppermint leaves.

Dried lavender (left) and dried and crushed peppermint leaves (right).

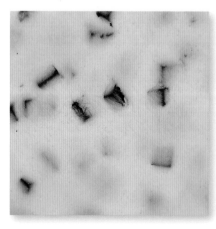

NON-ORGANIC INCLUSIONS

14 Chocolate chip cookie dough
Caramel-colored powder eye shadow; brown and champagne clay
How-to: Once cool, mix chunks of baked brown clay into raw champagne clay. Use sandpaper or a stiff brush to expose some of the chunks, then apply caramel-colored powder and bake (see page 27).

15 Foiled again

Gold and silver foil candy wrappers; translucent clay
How-to: Cut the foil wrappers into small pieces, mix into translucent clay, then bake and quench (see page 26).

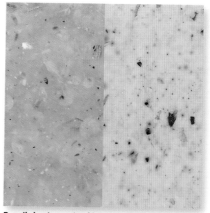

18 Close shave

Colored pencil shavings; translucent and white clay
How-to: Sharpen several colored pencils. Pick out any big pieces of wood, then mix the remaining colored shavings into the clay. Bake and quench. The pencil colors used here are green, light green, blue, light blue and purple (left) and yellow, red, blue, black and orange (right). To use crayons, peel off paper and sharpen the crayons. Mix the shavings into the clay as for pencils.

Pencil shavings mixed into translucent clay (left) and a 1:1 mix of translucent and white clay (right).

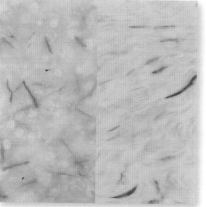

16 A stitch in time

Embroidery threads in various colors; translucent and champagne clay
How-to: Cut the embroidery threads into small pieces, about ⅛–¼in (3–6mm), and mix into the clay (see page 26). Combine several different shades of thread for added interest—here, three shades of red in translucent clay; and black, brown and gray threads in champagne clay.

Threads mixed into translucent clay (left) and champagne clay (right).

METALLIC POWDER

19 Hexagonal grid

Red mica powder; gold clay
How-to: Place masking material with all-over pattern (such as sequin scrap) onto a sheet of clay and use a sponge to apply mica powder over the top of both, then carefully remove the mask (see page 31).

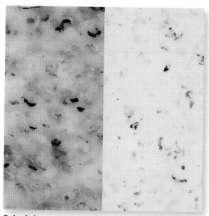

17 Linoleum

Multicolored baked clay scraps; translucent clay
How-to: Mix shavings, carving scraps and drill scraps of baked clay into translucent clay (see page 27). You can also mix them into white or any other light-colored clay. The specks of baked clay will show through and look like a 1960s linoleum tile.

Baked clay scraps mixed into translucent clay (left) and white clay (right).

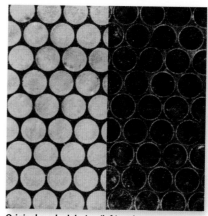

20 Dotted grid

Gold mica powder; black clay
How-to: Make in the same way as tile 19, applying gold mica powder to black clay. Then place the mask, reverse (powdered) side down, onto another sheet of black clay and press to transfer the leftover powder to the clay.

Original masked design (left) and reverse design (right).

21 Pearlized carving
Black acrylic paint and mica powder in several colors; translucent clay
How-to: Use the cutter carving technique to make a tile using translucent clay (see page 108). Use a fingertip to brush on mica powders and then bake (see page 31). When cool, apply a wash of black acrylic, then wipe off the excess to leave the paint just in the carved marks (see page 32).

See page 117 for alternative colorway.

Green man brooch
Dawn M. Schiller
A sculpted face is embellished with leaves and branches that are handbuilt and textured with a needle tool. The whole piece is brushed with copper mica powder before baking.

22 Lace rainbow
Mica powder in several colors; black clay
How-to: Roll out clay and press lace fabric or texture sheet onto it. Roll over the fabric to texture the clay. Lightly brush mica powders across the surface of the clay using a fingertip (see page 31).

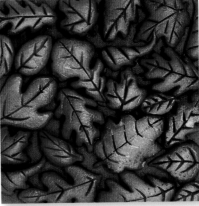

See page 135 for alternative colorway.

PAINTS & GLAZES

24 Autumn leaves
Brown and metallic acrylic paints; red clay
How-to: Make a stenciled leaves pavé tile and bake (see page 128). Apply a wash of brown acrylic all over, then rub it off the high spots with a cloth. Use a fingertip to brush on metallic highlights; copper and violet are used here (see page 32).

23 Aztec sun
Metallic rub-on wax in various colors; black clay
How-to: Use a rubber stamp to impress a design into a sheet of clay and then bake. When cool, use a fingertip to rub color onto raised areas of the design (as tile 22). Wax-based colorants give a softer, warmer color than mica powder. Waxes do not rub off easily, but you may wish to protect the surface finish with a sealant such as a gel medium or clear glaze.

Stained with brown paint (left) and metallic silver paint (right).

25 Rustic and aged
Brown and silver acrylic paints; champagne clay
How-to: Impress clay using stamps and needle tools. Apply a wash of acrylic paint, using a stencil brush to push the color into the indentations in the clay. Allow the paint to dry slightly, then wipe across the surface with a towel (see page 32).

26 Stenciled colors

Metallic acrylic paint, ink pad and mica powder; gold clay

How-to: Place punched paper stencils onto sheet of gold clay and apply various coloring mediums: acrylic paint, ink pad and mica powder (see page 31).

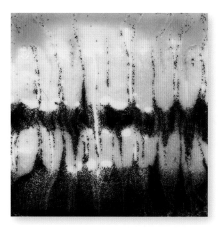

29 Shimmering glaze

Gold and pink mica powder and black embossing powder; liquid clay and baked white tile

How-to: Color the liquid clay with the powders to create thick dimensional glazes and apply in horizontal stripes to the tile. Drag a needle tool vertically through the colors in alternating directions (see page 113). Bake to set the liquid clay.

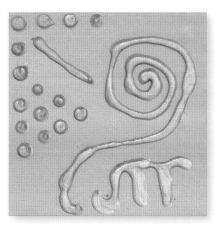

27 Dots and squiggles

Lumiere 3D fabric paint; gold clay

How-to: Apply paint to baked clay in any design you like and allow to dry (see page 33). Experiment with dots, lines, swirls and squiggles. Most fabric paints work well with polymer clay. The paint used here is dimensional, making it perfect for drawing raised designs, and also works as a glue for attaching extra embellishments.

METAL LEAF & FOIL

30 Old gold crackle

Gold metal leaf; black clay

How-to: For linear crackle, roll out the clay and apply a sheet of gold leaf to surface (see page 34). Pass clay through a pasta machine on the next thinnest setting or roll by hand. For square crackle, turn the sheet 90 degrees and roll again.

Linear crackle (left) and square crackle (right).

28 Sacred heart

Oil paints and mica powders in various colors; liquid clay and baked clay tile with 3D motif

How-to: Mix up several colors of liquid clay by adding a small amount of oil paint, then thin to a glaze-like consistency with mineral oil (see page 33). Paint the motif, then mix some mica powder into liquid clay and apply this to the background.

31 Scattered gold

Gold leaf; translucent and black clay

How-to: Apply gold leaf to translucent clay (see page 34) and roll out as thinly as you can. Lay the translucent clay gold side down onto a sheet of black clay. Use a roller to press the sheets together, then bake and quench.

32 Starry, starry night

Gold metal leaf; metallic black and opaque black clay

How-to: Roll out sheet of metallic clay, ⅛in (3mm) thick, and smaller sheet of opaque clay, ½in (1mm) thick. Apply gold leaf to smaller sheet (see page 34), then use a cutter to cut out small gold stars. Apply stars to larger clay sheet and then roll to impress the stars into the clay, starting gently and finishing when the combined sheet is ⅛in (3mm) thick.

35 Flower garlands

Silver foil; black clay

How-to: Roll out clay and impress with a rubber stamp. Apply a sheet of foil (see page 34). The ripped-off sheet of foil will have foil flower shapes on it where the foil has not stuck to the impressed clay; you can apply the silver flowers to another sheet of clay, as in tile 34.

33 Blue ice

Variegated foil; black clay

How-to: Roll out clay and use a rubber stamp to impress a design into the clay. Lay sheet of foil, colored side up, on top of the clay. Rub with fingers to warm up the foil. Scrape a tissue blade across the surface several times, then rip off foil quickly (see page 34). The foil will adhere to the raised areas of the clay.

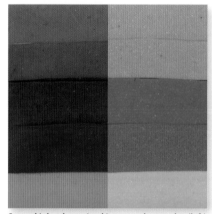

Several ink colors mixed into translucent clay (left) and pearl white clay (right).

ALCOHOL INK

36 Color blocks

Alcohol inks; translucent and pearl white clay

How-to: Apply ink to the clay surface, let the ink dry and then mix the dried ink into the clay (see page 35). All types of clay can be tinted with inks to change the color. The more translucent the clay, the stronger the color will be.

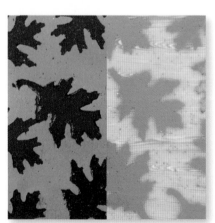

34 Oak leaves

Green foil; dark- and light-colored clay

How-to: Use a leaf-shaped paper punch to cut leaf stencils from copier paper. Lay stencils onto sheet of dark clay, then apply foil (see page 34). Gently lift off stencils to reveal bare clay beneath. The ripped-off sheet of foil will have foil leaf shapes on it where the stencils were on the clay. Lay the foil sheet onto a sheet of light clay and transfer the foil leaves to the clay as before.

Stenciled leaf design (left) and leftover foil leaves (right).

37 Dream face

Alcohol inks in various colors and rubbing alcohol; flesh-colored clay

How-to: Washes of alcohol inks mixed with rubbing alcohol in little containers or paper cups are brushed onto the clay surface as if painting with acrylic or oil paints.

Tile by Meta Strick.

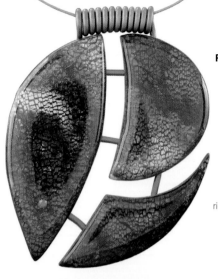

River delta pendant

Martina Medenica

This pendant is made from separate sections of polymer clay applied to an aluminum wire frame. The clay is covered with metal leaf, rolled to create a crackle effect and then colored with alcohol inks. After baking and cooling, a glossy coat of UV resin is applied, giving the piece beautiful richness and depth.

40 Lapis lazuli

Sapphire blue alcohol ink and gold metal leaf; translucent clay mixed with tiny amount of white clay

How-to: Mix alcohol ink into the clay, then apply a sheet of gold leaf and knead that into the clay (see page 35). Quench the baked clay to maximize transparency and reveal the gold inclusions deeper within the semiprecious stone.

38 Peacock enamel

Silver metal leaf, alcohol inks and UV resin; white clay

How-to: Roll out clay and apply sheet of silver leaf (see page 34). Impress with a rubber stamp and then color using alcohol inks (see page 35). A cool color palette of blues and greens are used here. Bake, allow to cool and then coat with resin.

41 Molten gold

Alcohol inks and mica powder; translucent clay

How-to: Roll out clay and apply red alcohol ink a drop at a time from the bottle, spreading the ink over the surface (see page 35). Add a few drops of yellow and white ink, letting them spread randomly into the red ink. Sprinkle mica powder onto the wet ink. The powder will absorb the ink to create pools of molten color.

39 Phoenix enamel

Silver metal leaf, alcohol inks and UV resin; white clay

How-to: Make in the same way as tile 38, but using a warm color palette of red, orange and tangerine inks.

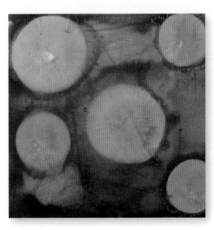

42 Drip, drip, drop

Alcohol inks and mica powder; translucent clay

How-to: Roll out clay and use a fingertip or soft brush to cover the surface with gold mica powder (see page 31). Apply green alcohol ink a drop at a time from the bottle, spreading the ink over the surface by tilting the tile and blowing the ink. Add a few drops of white ink on top (see page 35).

INCLUSIONS & ADDITIONS

Polymer clay artists at work

These pieces demonstrate just how exciting and varied inclusions and additions can be when used by artists. You will find mica powders mixed into or dusted onto the unbaked clay, sometimes with acrylic paints applied after baking for an antique look, or washed over with iridescent alcohol ink. As you will see, in the hands of skilled artists each medium can be applied in many different ways to create beautiful and highly individual results.

» See pages 36–43 for tile samples

▲ Fallen leaf pendant

Cindy Silas

Techniques used: A 2⅛ x 1¼in (5.5 x 3cm) leaf-shaped frame of sterling silver is embellished with a Skinner blend of polymer clay mixed with embossing powders. The shaded fall colors of the clay are given extra depth and richness by the inclusion of different-colored powders. The speckles of powder also give the clay an earthy, granular appearance that is beautifully contrasted by the sinuous frame of smooth silver.

See EMBOSSING POWDER tile 8

◄ Ganesha triptych

Doreen Kassel

Techniques used: A 3 x 3¼in (7.5 x 8cm) wooden triptych is covered with white polymer clay, then the figure of Ganesha is sculpted onto the triptych along with decorative embellishments. The piece is baked for only 15 minutes and then allowed to cool. The triptych is stained with a wash of burnt umber oil paint, which is then rubbed off to leave color only in the recesses and textured areas. Additional colors are then applied, some as washes and some painted onto the sculpture like a colored glaze. The finished triptych is fully baked to harden the polymer and set the oil paints permanently.

See PAINTS & GLAZES tiles 24 & 28 (but using oil paint only)

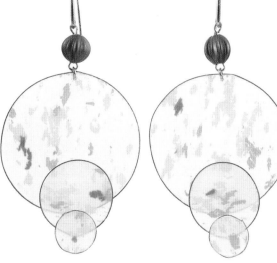

▶ See through earrings
Elvira Krick

Techniques used: Each 3in (7.5cm) long earring is composed of three polymer clay disks in graduating sizes attached to a bead and earwire. Each disk is made from a very thin circle of translucent clay with random splashes of oil pastel. Another thin circle of translucent traps the pastel inclusion between the two layers before being baked. Each clay disk is set inside a circle of terracotta-colored wire.

See NON-ORGANIC INCLUSIONS tiles 15–18 (but sandwiching the inclusions between layers of clay rather than kneading them in)

▼ Green goddess necklace
Marie Segal

Techniques used: Meso-American art was the inspiration for this 24in (60cm) long necklace with 3¼ x 1½in (8 x 4cm) focal bead. Verdigris embossing powder is mixed into translucent clay before the beads and main pendant are cut and shaped. A thin sheet of black clay covered with gold leaf is used to make embellishments, along with slices of leaf and heart cane. The gold leaf is protected from tarnishing with a thin coat of lacquer.

See EMBOSSING POWDER tile 8, PAINTS & GLAZES tiles 24–25 and METAL LEAF & FOIL tile 30

◀ Twist and shout necklace
Helen Breil

Techniques used: All of the components in this necklace are polymer clay except for the black spacer beads. Mica powders are applied to the clay before baking, and then lime green and turquoise Viva Decor Inka Gold metallic acrylic paint (which comes in an easy-to-apply paste form) is brushed on afterward. A custom-made texture sheet is used on the three spiral feature beads. The largest spiral bead measures 2¾ x 1½in (7 x 4cm).

See METALLIC POWDER tiles 21–22 and PAINTS & GLAZES tile 24

◄ Spring fever earrings

Anke Humpert

Techniques used: A 2in (5cm) diameter white polymer clay bead core is decorated with colored pencils and then covered with two or three thin layers of translucent clay, some partly covered with gold foil or leaf for extra richness, to build up a glazed effect (see also page 68). This glazing protects the color decoration and can also be sanded and buffed to a shine if desired. The circular patterns drawn onto the clay beads are echoed by the three metal washers tinted with alcohol inks hanging above.

See METAL LEAF & FOIL tiles 30–31 & 34 and ALCOHOL INK tiles 41–42

► Faux batik brooch

Pavla Čepelíková

Techniques used: Different shapes made out of polymer clay are painted with several layers and patterns of alcohol ink to simulate the wax-resist dyed patterns on batik textiles. The lightest layer of color is applied first, followed by the darker layers. Various shapes are then combined to create brooches, pendants and earrings. This brooch comprises four leaf shapes joined with three small disks, all in graduating sizes. The brooch measures 2 x 2in (5 x 5cm) at its widest points.

See ALCOHOL INK tiles 37 & 41–42

◄ Heart choker

Marie Segal

Techniques used: Wonderful, shimmering mica powders are mixed into the clay to create the cylindrical and twisted tube beads, which are made using an extruder. These clay beads are interspersed with store-bought glass millefiori and flat acrylic beads to make up the 19in (48cm) long necklace. The 1¼in (3cm) heart is impressed on both sides with a rubber stamp, then several colors of mica powder are applied to give the appearance of raku ware or aurora borealis. The bead on the heart is threaded onto wire and embedded into the clay (see page 144).

See METALLIC POWDER tiles 21–22

► Terra nova bowl

Andrijana Katavić

Techniques used: This beautiful 4¾in (12cm) diameter bowl is made in the ceramic tradition but using new mediums to simulate the look of real glazed ceramic. The sculpted polymer clay bowl is textured with a custom-made texture sheet and then painted with acrylic paints and inks and liquid clay glazes. The decorated bowl is then covered with a marine varnish mixed with a little bit of resin.

See PAINTS & GLAZES tiles 24 & 28–29 and ALCOHOL INK tiles 41–42

▼ Crayon lei

Lindly Haunani

Techniques used: Crayon shavings and pieces of linen thread are mixed into translucent clay to produce soft pastel colors with the look of frosted glass. Various bead shapes are sculpted and then pierced so that the leaves and blossoms hang down when worn. The fact that something as basic as a child's crayon can be used to produce such an effective design is testament to the wide-ranging compatibility of polymer clay. The loop on the closure is made from flexible polymer clay. The necklace is 26in (66cm) long.

See NON-ORGANIC INCLUSIONS tiles 16 & 18

◄ Chainmail statement necklace

Leila Bidler

Techniques used: This 18in (46cm) long necklace is made to resemble the linked rings of chainmail armor but using rings of extruded polymer clay woven together. First a sheet of silver leaf is applied to the clay, which is then run though a pasta machine repeatedly until the leaf is broken into tiny pieces, almost as fine as glitter, and distributed evenly throughout the clay to give the rings a subtle metallic sparkle. Ground black pepper is also added to the mix for contrast. The necklace is about 1in (2.5cm) thick at the front.

See ORGANIC INCLUSIONS tile 11 and METAL LEAF & FOIL tile 31

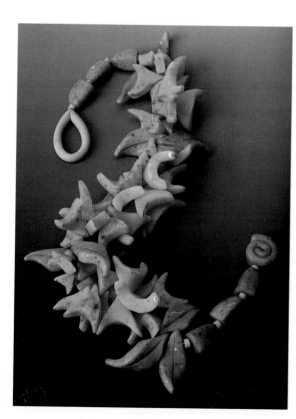

► Cake topper

Dawn Stubitsch

Techniques used: The artist sculpts the wedding couple out of polymer clay, using reference photographs to create an amazingly realistic representation of the couple in the clothes they intend to wear. Everything is made from polymer clay except for a few details like the veil. The faces are the most time-consuming element to create, and require magnifying glasses and tiny tools. Facial features such as eyes, eyebrows and lips are also painted, and liquid clay tinted with a heat-set oil paint is used to paint lace designs on the dress if appropriate. A dusting of mica powder simulates satin fabric. Glitter is glued onto the dress if more glitz is needed, and tiny crystals and glitter are applied to the polymer clay jewelry for sparkle. The topper is about 7in (18cm) high.

See GLITTER tile 3, METALLIC POWDER tiles 21–22 and PAINTS & GLAZES tile 28

TEXTURE EFFECTS

Applying texture

Polymer clay takes the impression of whatever it is pressed against. You can press the clay onto the texturing material or vice versa, use a roller to press the clay and material together, or pass flexible texturing materials through a pasta machine with the clay. As well as using texture sheets, rubber stamps and texturing tools designed for polymer clay, you can also texture clay using all sorts of other materials and objects, including textiles, leaves and grasses.

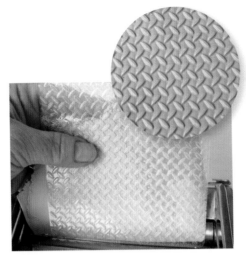

Commercial texture sheet
Also known as texture plates, these are widely available in numerous designs. Spray a light mist of water onto the texture sheet to prevent sticking. Roll out a sheet of clay, ⅛in (3mm) thick, and place it against the misted side of the texture sheet. Roll both pieces together through a pasta machine on the thickest setting or use a roller.

Improvised texture sheet
You can use all sorts of materials in the same way as a commercial texture sheet, such as corrugated cardboard. Place the cardboard, textured side down, onto the clay. Lightly roll over the cardboard to set the grooves in place, then roll again with a bit more pressure to impress the clay.

You will need:

- Polymer clay, pasta machine, roller and tissue blade

- Texturing materials, including ready-made commercial texture sheets, corrugated cardboard, fabric, lace and unmounted rubber stamps

- Aluminum foil, sheet of packing foam, gel medium and tongue depressor

- Dried or fresh leaves and grasses plus talcum powder or cornstarch

- Coarse-grit sandpaper and mask made using paper punches and cardstock

- Variety of hand tools, such as ball stylus, cutters and carving tools

Aluminum foil
1 You can texture aluminum foil and then apply it to polymer clay. Lay a sheet of foil and then packing foam on top of a texture sheet. Roll through a pasta machine on the thickest setting. Fill the impressed areas on the back of the foil with gel medium, using a tongue depressor (or similar tool) to spread the gel. Do not press on the foil—fill the impressions, don't flatten them.

2 Allow the gel to dry completely. You may need to apply another coat of gel if the impressions are really deep. Roll out some clay and trim to the required size, then cut out a piece of foil the same size. Paint the back of the foil with a thin coat of gel medium (to act as a glue), press the foil gently onto the clay and then bake. Textured foil can be cut into various shapes to make embellishments.

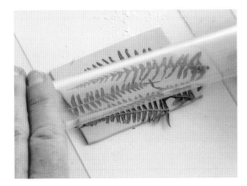

Natural materials

1 Natural leaves and grasses make wonderful textures. If using dried materials, roll out a sheet of clay, ⅛in (3mm) thick, and sprinkle with talcum powder or cornstarch to prevent sticking. Lay the leaves onto the clay, then roll firmly over them to impress the texture into the clay. If using fresh materials, mist the clay lightly with water to prevent sticking.

2 Remove the leaves from the clay. You can use a needle tool or tweezers to remove any tiny bits of leaves if they do stick in the impressed areas. Cut the clay into the required shape and then bake. Alternatively, bake the whole thing and use it as a texture sheet for impressing other pieces of clay with the design.

Impressions of nature pendant
Kelly Steindorf

The clay is impressed with fresh lavender leaves and then cut into shape and baked. Using fresh leaves rather than dried means that the pliable leaves can be shaped on the clay as desired. The impressed design is stained with earth-toned acrylic paint and the pendant is hung from a hand-forged copper chain. The finished piece looks more like earthen clay than polymer clay.

Textile effects

1 You can use polymer clay to simulate textiles by texturing thin sheets of clay with real fabric. Choose a fabric with a clear weave to get a good imprint, and roll the clay ⅟₃₂in (1mm) thick or less so that it can be folded and draped. Dampen the fabric to prevent sticking, then pass it through a pasta machine with the clay. Alternatively, place the damp fabric onto the clay and use a roller to impress the texture.

2 Try using a strip of lace to texture polymer clay. The thin clay can be cut out with a scalloped edge (do this freehand or using a scalloped cookie cutter) and then gathered into frills.

Doll in lace dress
Sue Heaser

This polymer clay doll is wearing a dress, lace petticoat and ribbon all made in polymer clay. Using real fabrics and lace to texture the clay gives a touch of realism to this whimsical piece and makes a simple idea blossom into something quite delightful.

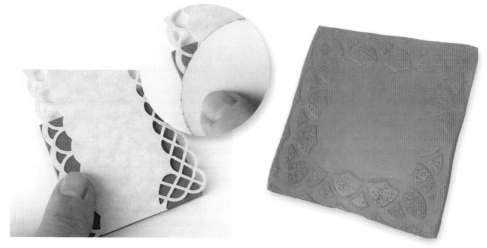

Sandpaper

1 Press coarse-grit sandpaper onto the clay to create a stippled texture that looks like blacktop (especially in black clay). You can use a roller to impress larger areas, or bend the paper around your fingers to press onto smaller areas. Flexible sanding pads are ideal for this, or cut a sheet of sandpaper into smaller pieces.

2 Texturing the clay through punched paper masks is an easy way to make small textured frames for bordering images or focal pieces. Lightly press the mask onto the clay, then use sandpaper to apply texture through the spaces. A mask with two different border designs is used here, so take care only to texture the spaces through the design you are using.

3 When you have finished texturing the first edge of the clay, peel off the mask and press it along the next edge of the clay. Texture through the spaces as before, then repeat around each edge of the clay to complete the border.

Purple leaves brooches

Dayle Doroshow

These brooches are made using blended sheets of purple and green clay with an all-over stippled texture. Stippling can be applied in various ways, such as with sandpaper or a stiff brush. A blade is used to mark additional lines for the leaf veins, and the designs are accented with thin twisted logs and indented balls of clay.

Rubber stamps

1 Place a rubber stamp onto the clay and press down to make a deep impression. If using raw clay, spray a mist of water or other release agent onto the stamp first to prevent sticking (see page 13). Here, the clay is covered with silver leaf and this will prevent sticking. Gently peel away the stamp to reveal the impression in the clay, then continue stamping the clay as required.

2 Most rubber stamps have a defined image or pattern, but you can still use them to create a general all-over texture. Bend an unmounted rubber stamp over your forefinger and press a small section into the clay. Repeat across the whole surface of the clay. Here, you can see pieces of the stamp's spiral design, but they will overlap to create a random texture that is not really a definite pattern.

Hand tools

1 Almost anything can be used as a texture tool, not just tools designed for the purpose, so try out a variety of objects to see what kind of marks you can make with them. Here, the edge of a seashell is pressed into the clay, and then a ball stylus is used to impress dots along the scalloped lines of the shell. Ball styluses come in several sizes and are a valuable tool in the clay artist's toolbox.

2 Different tools can be used to create the same texture marks. A U-shaped carving tool can be pressed straight up and down into the clay to create a pattern that could be used to simulate anything from fish scales to dragonskin. A small round cutter can be used to make a similar design. Hold the cutter at an angle so that only the bottom edge impresses the clay.

Seka segment cuff
Martina Medenica
Segments veneered with faux ikat and striped canes are interspersed with segments that have been textured with a variety of tools and then stained with black and white acrylic paint for an aged look.

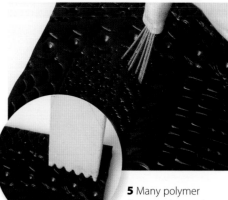

3 Use cutters to impress shapes into the clay—circles, teardrops, flowers, stars and so on. Improvise with other objects, such as a fan pull ball chain. Use the end to impress circles and the chain to impress dots (see page 126 for impressing an all-over dot pattern into clay).

4 Try using other objects that you have lying around your home—a small luggage key, for example. Tools that you use for another craft may also work well with polymer clay, such as the loop tool used for trimming ceramic pots. Keep trying out different tools to see their effects—like doodling on paper but this time on polymer clay.

5 Many polymer clay texturing tools are designed to help you work more quickly and easily. There are tools for applying lines of "stitching" or for stippling clay with many holes simultaneously.

TEXTURE EFFECTS

Making a texture sheet

Although texture sheets are widely available to buy, it is easy to make your own using silicone molding compound. A silicone texture sheet is durable and most can even be baked, which is useful when working with liquid clay. The thinner you make the texture sheet, the more flexible it will be, allowing you to wrap the sheet around different shapes as well as texture flat pieces of clay.

Silicone texture sheet

1 Measure out equal quantities of the two colors of molding compound as directed on the package—1 tbsp (15ml) of each should be sufficient to make a thinly rolled 5in (12.5cm) square texture sheet. Wipe the spoon before measuring the second part of the molding compound to avoid cross-contamination.

2 Mix the two different-colored putties together for about a minute or according to the directions. Do not mix too vigorously—the more heat that gets into the compound, the faster it will set and the less working time you will have to make the mold. Once the mixture is a uniform color, the compound is ready to use.

You will need:

- Polymer clay and roller
- Two-part putty silicone molding compound and measuring spoon
- Flat textured plastic tablecloth with cutout pattern or similar item to be molded
- Bamboo skewer or needle tool (optional)

3 Roll out a log of the mixture, slightly longer than the width of the area you want to mold, and position it just below the area to be molded.

Faux crocodile leather earrings

Saskia Veltenaar

Sections of textured clay are joined with jump rings to make articulated earrings. There are many ways of simulating realistic animal skin textures like this, including impressing the clay with a suitable texture sheet (as here) or with real or faux crocodile leather.

4 Starting at the bottom of the log, roll away from you and upward. Then roll the sides outward; the compound will spread quite far. If you see any air bubbles (they show as bumps), try to roll them out. Do not try to lift the putty to expel the bubbles; the putty is not solid enough to do that and you will have a hard time placing it back down in the same place.

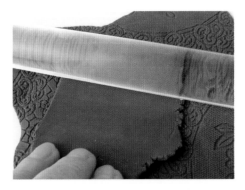

5 To make a more flexible texture sheet, keep rolling until you start to see an impression of the pattern. (You can do this with plastic tablecloths or any material where the textured surface is not sharp.) If you see any thicker areas, roll from the center outward to thin them out, but be careful not to roll the compound too thinly; you will get better with practice. Don't lift the edges to check the other side or you may spoil the pattern.

6 If you wish, use a bamboo skewer or needle tool to inscribe your name and the date on the reverse. You can tell when the compound has set when you can press a fingernail into it and it leaves no mark. Wait another five minutes to be completely sure and then peel back the mold to reveal the detailed impression of the tablecloth pattern on the front of the texture sheet.

7 To use the texture sheet, mist the sheet with water so that the clay will release easily. Lay a sheet of clay on top of the texture sheet (or vice versa) and use a roller to roll across them. Carefully peel back the clay to reveal the impressed texture.

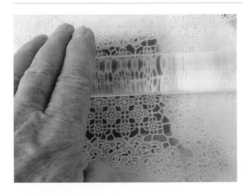

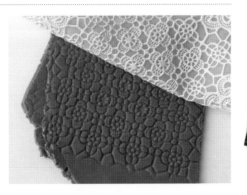

Original material

1 You can use the original tablecloth (or other chosen material) as a ready-made texture sheet. Lay the cloth over a sheet of clay, making sure that the textured area you want to impress into the clay is positioned over the clay. Roll over the clay, taking care that the cloth does not slip out of place while doing so.

2 Peel back the tablecloth, revealing the texture on the clay. If you discover that you have not positioned the tablecloth correctly or have not impressed the texture evenly into the clay, simply recondition the clay and start again.

Same material, different look
The silicone texture sheet will replicate the original tablecloth pattern in the clay (top), while using the tablecloth itself as a texture sheet will impress the clay with the reverse of the pattern (bottom). Both samples have been highlighted with mica powder.

TEXTURE EFFECTS

Texture sticks and paddles

A texture stick is a rod of clay into which a metal bead or other texturing object is embedded. Use the same principle to make a needle tool for scoring lines into clay. Texture paddles are a simple way of applying an all-over texture that can be subtle or strong, depending on the material used to make the paddle.

You will need:

- Scrap polymer clay, roller and tissue blade
- Round-nose pliers, wire cutters and scissors
- Metal beads, headpins and sharp needle
- At least 40in (1m) length of texturing material, such as cording, yarn, chain, wire or fused plastic pearls
- 3 x 1½in (7.5 x 4cm) pieces of chipboard, cardboard, wood or plastic (or use scrap polymer clay)

Bead texture sticks
These are useful for impressing small textural design details into clay. Choose metal beads so that they retain their shape during baking.

Texture stick
1 Thread a metal bead onto a headpin. Using round-nose pliers, bend the pin back and forth just below the bead, then turn a loop in the wire. Trim the crimped wire to about 1in (2.5cm) long.

3 Work the clay around the end of the headpin. Press the clay under and around the bead so that the base of the bead is embedded in the clay handle. Roll the handle to smooth over the seam. Check that the bead is straight and the headpin is centered in the bead. If the handle is too big after rolling it, cut off the excess and then bake.

2 Roll a 1in (2.5cm) ball of scrap clay, then roll it into a log about 2in (5cm) long. Use a blade to cut a channel along one end of the log, cutting about halfway through. Lay the crimped headpin into the channel, making sure that the bead is at the very end of the pin. Close the clay around the headpin.

Owl brooch
Sue Heaser
The bird is textured with scored lines to indicate feathers, with heavier scoring on the body to simulate the thick, downy feathers there. Washes of acrylic paint over translucent clay give a porcelain effect.

Needle tool
You can purchase many different types of needle tool or you can make your own. Simply insert a needle into a rod of clay or glue it into a hole drilled into a piece of wooden dowel. The handle makes it easier to manipulate the tool.

Cord texture paddle

1 Roll out a sheet of clay, ⅛in (3mm) thick. Cut out a 2in (5cm) square of clay for each texture paddle you are making and bake. Leaving a tail end for tying a knot, wrap the texturing material (cord is used here) diagonally over the top of the tile, holding the tail end of the cord in place with your thumb.

2 Now wrap the long end of the cord vertically around the clay tile. Take it over the top of the tile, right next to the first wrap you made. Continue wrapping the cord vertically around the tile, keeping the wraps tight against each other and covering the diagonal tail end of the cord.

Take care not to press too deeply or the texturing material may stick to the clay.

Ancient texturing tools

Our ancestors used texture paddles when making clay pots. They would make pots out of coils of clay and then paddle them out to thinner, different shapes. There have been studies done on the migration of peoples by the textures they used on ceramic ware. It is easy to replicate this ancient tool for use with polymer clay. All sorts of materials can be used to create the texture, including yarn, thread, string, cording, chain, leather, fused plastic pearls or any pliable wire (such as telephone wire). Yarn and string probably most resemble the paddles of ancient times. The paddle itself can be made from baked clay, wood, plastic, cardboard or chipboard. As well as wrapping materials around the paddle to create texture, you can also carve textural designs into a wooden or polymer clay paddle.

3 Pulling the cord as tightly as possible around the tile, tie the two ends of the cord together in a knot. Trim off the excess. The knotted side is the back of the texture paddle. Push all of the cords together on the front of the paddle.

4 To use the paddle, place it over the raw polymer clay and press down. You can press with the fingers, palm or heel of the hand. Reposition the paddle and make more marks randomly on the clay as required.

Notch

Yarn texture paddle

You can make a texture paddle using a variety of materials. This one is llama yarn wrapped around a piece of chipboard. You can cut notches in the sides of the chipboard to hold the ends of the yarn instead of tying them in a knot.

Notch

TEXTURE EFFECTS

Tile samples

Texture is one of the easiest ways to change the look of polymer clay because the clay picks up impressions extremely well, forming a perfect copy of whatever you press against it. You can buy ready-made texture sheets and rubber stamps in a wide variety of designs, but you can also use other materials and tools to apply texture. Lace, fabric and paper products can all be used for texturing clay, as well as all sorts of miscellaneous items that you will already have around your home or workshop—knitting needles, paperclips, carving tools, sewing wheels, paintbrush handles and so on.

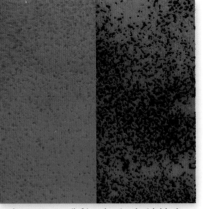

Sandpaper texture (left) and stained with black acrylic (right).

SANDPAPER

1 Stippled texture
Black acrylic paint; red clay
How-to: Press sandpaper over the surface of the clay to give it an all-over texture (see page 50). Apply a wash of black acrylic, then wipe off the excess with a cloth. Also try other color combinations of clay and paint. Other tools you can use to create a stippled texture include a stencil brush, toothbrush or nail brush.

2 Textured frame
Black acrylic paint; silver clay
How-to: Apply a mask along one edge of the clay (a punched paper mask is used here) and use sandpaper to texture the clay through the mask; repeat along each edge of the clay (see page 50). Apply a wash of black acrylic, then wipe off the excess with a cloth.

Pirate treasure seahorse
Leila Bidler
A real dried seahorse is molded and then raw clay pressed into the mold to produce a realistic replica. You can make highly detailed molds using putty silicone molding compound or polymer clay itself. This seahorse has been painted with Swellegant metal coating and rust patina to give the seahorse the look of rusted metal—perfect for a piece of pirate treasure.

Brown clay stained with black acrylic (left) and green clay stained with gold acrylic (right).

3 Scratching the surface
Black and gold acrylic paint; brown and green clay
How-to: Bake a sheet of clay and sand with a coarse-grit sandpaper; 80-grit paper is used here. You can leave the textured clay as it is, or apply a wash of acrylic paint and wipe off the excess to accentuate the scratched lines.

TEXTURE SHEETS & STAMPS

4 Metallic grid

Silver mica powder and black acrylic paint; silver clay

How-to: Use a texture sheet to impress a sheet of clay (see page 48). Use a fingertip to rub silver powder across the raised areas of texture, then bake and allow to cool. Apply a wash of black acrylic, then wipe off the excess.

5 Arabian nights

Black and gold acrylic paint; confetti dots cane (see tile 12, page 96) and white clay

How-to: Apply a thin slice of the cane to a sheet of white clay. Impress with a texture sheet and then bake (see page 48). Apply a wash of black acrylic and then wipe off the excess. Use a fingertip to brush on gold acrylic highlights.

6 Anodized aluminum

Aluminum foil, gel medium and baja blue and lime-green alcohol ink; black clay

How-to: Texture the foil using a texture sheet and then fill the impressed areas on the back of the foil with gel medium (see page 48). When dry, cut the foil to shape, attach it to a sheet of black clay with more gel medium and then bake. Color the foil with alcohol ink (see page 35).

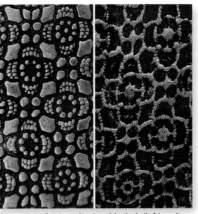

Clay textured using plastic tablecloth (left) and texture sheet made from the cloth (right).

7 Four-square flower

Gold mica powder; brown clay

How-to: Make a silicone texture sheet from a plastic tablecloth or other textured sheet material (see page 52). Use both the tablecloth and the texture sheet to texture sheets of clay. Use a fingertip to rub a little mica powder over the raised areas of the clay.

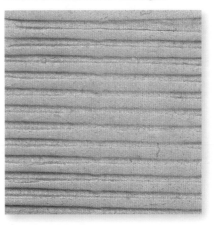

8 Corrugated cardboard

Silver clay

How-to: Place some corrugated cardboard onto a sheet of clay and use a roller to impress the texture into the clay (see page 48). Most paper products are too absorbent to use with polymer clay because they absorb the plasticizer and stick, but you can usually use cardboard several times before it becomes unusable.

Two different woven fabrics impressed into clay.

9 Fabric weave

Green and orange clay

How-to: Mist the fabric with water to prevent sticking, and then use it to texture sheets of clay using either a pasta machine or roller (see page 49). Choose fabrics with a clear weave and avoid fluffy or hairy fabrics.

10 Metallic paisley
White clay covered with silver leaf (see page 34)
How-to: Press a rubber stamp onto a sheet of leaf-covered clay (see page 50). Make sure that the stamp does not slip and press deeply to get a clear impression. Move the stamp to the next plain area of clay and repeat until the whole surface is textured. Try using the textured silver clay to simulate enamel (see page 35).

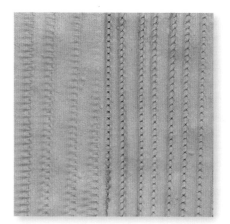

13 Texture illusion
1 part silver mica clay mixed with 1 part translucent
How-to: Utilize mica shift effects (see page 104) to create a tile that looks textured but is actually smooth. Roll out a sheet of clay and fold in half. Press the bristles of a brush (a steel pet comb is used here) into the clay and then roll flat. Bake and quench. The clay will be smooth to the touch but look textured.

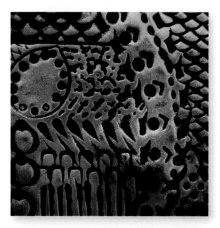

HAND TOOLS

11 Raku ware
Mica powders in various colors; black clay
How-to: Use a range of tools to impress a random textured pattern into a sheet of clay, from a seashell and luggage key to a ball stylus and stippling tool (see page 51). Use a fingertip to rub mica powders over the surface, allowing the impressed areas to remain black.

Tile by Kelly Steindorf.

NATURAL MATERIALS

14 Green world
Green and blue acrylic paints; white clay
How-to: Place dried leaves, flowers, seedheads or weeds onto a sheet of clay and use a roller to impress their texture into the clay (see page 49). Bake and allow to cool, then apply thin washes of acrylic paint.

12 Carved jade
Dried sage and brown acrylic paint; translucent clay
How-to: Mix sage into translucent clay, roll out and bake (see tile 13, page 38). Use a V-shaped carving tool to carve a design into the baked clay. Stain with brown acrylic and wipe off the excess with an old towel.

Tile by Kelly Steindorf.

15 Forest floor
Brown acrylic paint; champagne clay
How-to: Make in the same way as tile 14, but using fresh lavender leaves so that you can manipulate the leaves into a variety of shapes. After baking, stain with brown acrylic for an antiqued or aged look.

Texture marks (left) and with acrylic wash (right).

TEXTURE PADDLES

16 Llama yarn

White acrylic paint; brown clay
How-to: Make a texture paddle using a length of yarn (llama yarn is used here) and use it to give the clay an all-over texture (see page 55). Apply a wash of white acrylic, then wipe off the excess with a cloth. Try other yarn fibers and thicknesses, as well as string.

Texture marks on brown clay (left) and with acrylic wash on silver clay (right).

17 Snake chain

Black acrylic paint; brown and silver clay
How-to: Make in the same way as tile 16 but using a length of snake chain. Apply a wash of black acrylic, then wipe off the excess with a cloth. Snake chain works well for texture paddles because it is very tight-linked and will not get stuck in the clay too much, but do experiment with other types of chain (see tile 19).

18 Cording

Brown acrylic paint; brown and ocher clay
How-to: Make in the same way as tile 16 but using a length of cording. Apply a wash of brown acrylic, then wipe off the excess with a cloth. Experiment with cording in different widths and materials.

Texture marks (left) and with acrylic wash (right).

19 Faceted chain

Black acrylic paint; silver clay
How-to: This tile is the same as tile 17 but uses a faceted chain instead of a snake chain. Again, it is tight-linked to reduce the risk of tearing the clay if the chain gets stuck too deeply when the paddle is being used, but the faceting creates much more broken lines of texture than the snake chain.

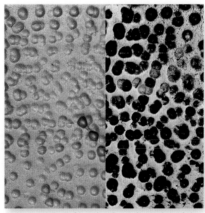

Texture marks (left) and with acrylic wash (right).

20 Fused pearls

Black acrylic paint; silver clay
How-to: Make in the same way as tile 16 but using a string of fused pearls (sold as a trimming at notions stores and craft stores). It is much easier to create this texture with a paddle than one dot at a time with a ball stylus.Apply a wash of black acrylic, then wipe off the excess with a cloth.

Texture marks on silver clay (left) and with acrylic wash on yellow clay (right).

21 Spiral stamp

Black acrylic paint; silver and yellow clay
How-to: Use a flexible rubber stamp as a ready-made texture paddle. This one has a spiral design, but instead of pressing the stamp cleanly into the clay to replicate the spiral pattern, press small sections of the stamp onto the clay randomly so that the spirals overlap to create an all-over texture (see page 50). Apply a wash of black acrylic, then wipe off the excess with a cloth.

TEXTURE EFFECTS

Polymer clay artists at work

Texture can play a major part in the creation of successful polymer clay designs, from deeply impressed patterns using stamps and hand tools to creating a more subtle texture by using a coarse-grit sandpaper to sand the clay after baking. Textures can also be vital for giving faux pieces an authentic feel. The artists featured here employ a variety of methods to create a wide range of textural effects, and show how different textures can be combined to create a cohesive piece of design.

» See pages 56–59 for tile samples

◄ **Merwoman's necklace**
Randee M. Ketzel

Techniques used: Faux limestone polymer clay beads are strung with genuine abalone, stone and glass beads to make this wonderful sea-themed necklace. The limestone texture is created using a variety of natural and artificial materials. You could try combining sandpaper, texture paddles and needle tools to create stone-like textures. Various shells, stones, pearls and beads are also pressed into the limestone clay; some are left embedded in the clay, while others are removed to leave just their impressions for another layer of textural interest. After baking, the 1–1¼in (2.5–3cm) long limestone beads are antiqued with brown-toned acrylic mediums.
See SANDPAPER tile 1, HAND TOOLS tile 11, NATURAL MATERIALS tiles 14–15 and TEXTURE PADDLES tile 20

▲ **Pear book**
Cathy Johnston

Techniques used: Rubber stamps are used to apply a background texture of old writing to the polymer clay covers of this 2½ x 1½in (6.5 x 4cm) book, and then a pictorial stamp is pressed on top and the design is colored with chalk inks. The covers and pages of the book are tied together with waxed linen cords embellished with polymer clay beads in the shape of tiny pears.
See TEXTURE SHEETS & STAMPS tile 10

▶ **Pond box**
Helen Wyland-Malchow

Techniques used: After baking, the body of this slab-constructed box is textured by sanding and carving. The lid is a mokumé gané veneer created using a handcut mold to distort the layers of clay (see page 92). The veneer is also leached (made firmer by leaching out some of the plasticizer in the clay) so that it crackles when rolled more thinly. The shaped edge of the lid, offset glass rock knob and shiny plastic button feet all help to build up additional layers of texture in the design.
See SANDPAPER tile 3 and HAND TOOLS tiles 11–12

▶ Circles pendant
Cindy Silas

Techniques used: A custom-made texture sheet is used to impress a design into the silver metal clay dome of this 1⅜in (3.5cm) diameter pendant. The four spaces in the dome are filled with black polymer clay with a random dot texture. Mica powders mixed with gel medium are applied to the raised areas of the clay to accentuate the texture. The whole piece is tied together by the contrasting textures and metallic finishes.
See TEXTURE SHEETS & STAMPS tile 7 and TEXTURE PADDLES tile 20

◀ Tropical flower brooch
Dayle Doroshow

Techniques used: The outer petals of this 5in (12.5cm) diameter flower are cut from sheets of clay in blended colors to which a stippled texture is added using 180-grit sandpaper. The inner petals are cut from layered clay and carved with a few incised marks to reveal the underlying layer. Additional texture is created with tiny indented balls of clay and an antique brass button at the center.
See SANDPAPER tile 1 and HAND TOOLS tiles 11–12

◀ Quilted teapot
Kathryn Jo Ottman

Techniques used: A ceramic teapot is embellished with clay sheets that have been rolled through a pasta machine with texture sheets in different designs. The clay pieces are then patchworked together on the surface of the teapot in a crazy quilt style. The clay-covered teapot is baked in an oven, allowed to cool and then stained with acrylic paints to enhance and define the textured patterns.
See TEXTURE SHEETS & STAMPS tiles 4–5 & 7

▶ Textured pins

Andrijana Katavić

Techniques used: These pins are wonderful examples of how you can use all sorts of objects to texture polymer clay. The turquoise hair pin is textured using a lace tablecloth (flower pattern on the left), the sole of a slipper (circles at the center) and part of an old manual meat grinder and medical gauze (polka dots on the right). The ivory shawl pin is textured using a piece of wall from a building. Both pins are stained to accentuate the texture (acrylic paint on the turquoise pin, and gold patina for antique furniture on the ivory pin). The turquoise pin is about 2¾in (7cm) wide, and the ivory pin about 2in (5cm).

See TEXTURE SHEETS & STAMPS tiles 7 & 9 and HAND TOOLS tiles 11–12

▼ Saxon bronze necklace

Randee M. Ketzel

Techniques used: The faux bronze polymer clay beads of this 18in (46cm) long necklace are decorated with a variety of stamped designs and then colored and antiqued with iridescent, metallic and mica finishes, overlaid with acrylic paint. The focal bead features a faux opal cabochon embedded in a textured clay bezel and all the beads are strung together on an antiqued chain. The choice of stamped designs and the antiqued patinas give this piece a feeling of age but in a new medium.

See TEXTURE SHEETS & STAMPS tile 10 and HAND TOOLS tile 11

◀ Gold leaf textured necklace

Helen Breil

Techniques used: A sheet of variegated gold leaf is applied to black polymer clay and then textured using an anti-slip tread tape. Viva Decor Inka Gold metallic acrylic paint is applied on the edges of the pendant; this paint comes in paste form, which is easier to apply and control for this type of edge treatment. The gold nugget texture of the clay is combined with smooth and ridged metal beads and black velvet and twisted silk cords for a bold statement piece. The pendant measures 3¼ x 1½in (8 x 4cm).

See SANDPAPTER tile 1 and TEXTURE SHEETS & STAMPS tile 8

◄ **Juke joint**

Lisa Mathews

Techniques used: Hand-sculpted polymer clay figures are mounted on a painted background and framed in a 29½ x 53½ x 6in (75 x 136 x 15cm) shadow box. A glittery dress, a flowing skirt, the drape of the fabric on the pants and a puff of feathers all add a sense of movement and action to the sculpted and textured pictorial.

See SANDPAPER tile 1, TEXTURE SHEETS & STAMPS tile 9 and HAND TOOLS tiles 11–12

► **Civil rights chess set**

Lisa Mathews

Techniques used: These hand-sculpted figures form part of a chess set featuring caricatures of real life civil rights leaders, with opposing playing pieces representing the nonviolent versus radical civil rights movements (the pieces shown here represent the radical leaders). Many different textures are combined to create the individual hairstyles, facial features, clothes and shoes. The pieces are 8–12in (20–30cm) high.

See SANDPAPER tile 1, TEXTURE SHEETS & STAMPS tile 9 and HAND TOOLS tiles 11–12

PRINTING EFFECTS

Ink printing

Working with stamps is one of the most basic ways of printing onto polymer clay. By using an ink that dries completely on the surface of the clay, you can continue to manipulate the clay after the ink has dried. You will need to use a permanent ink such as StazOn, Brilliance or Archival, which deliver the ink nicely onto most surfaces and are permanent once dry.

You will need:

- Polymer clay in light or semi-translucent colors such as champagne and flesh
- Pasta machine or roller and tissue blade
- Selection of rubber stamps and permanent ink pads
- For making stamps:
  » Cutters and texturing tools
  » Small piece of glass (such as from a picture frame)
- For making tube beads (overleaf):
  » Bamboo skewer, 3/32in (2mm) thick
  » Masking tape, 3/4–1in (2–2.5cm) wide (use regular off-white masking tape; blue low-tack tape is used here for clarity)
  » Thin sheet of packing foam

Check through the glass to make sure there are no air bubbles between the glass and the fish.

Making stamps

1 Roll out some clay, 1/8in (3mm) thick, and use a cutter to cut out the shape of stamp you wish to make. Add detail as desired. Here, the fish's eye is cut out using a small teardrop cutter, the cutter is then used to impress scales on the fish's body (hold the cutter at an angle so that only the rounded edge touches the clay) and the mouth and tail are marked with a blade.

2 Lay the fish face down onto a sheet of glass. Very lightly press a finger onto the fish, starting at one end and working toward the other so that any air bubbles trapped between the clay and the glass are expelled. You can lift the front of the fish as you press along the body to help release them. Air bubbles need to be removed so that the fish is perfectly flat for even printing. Turn the glass over to double-check.

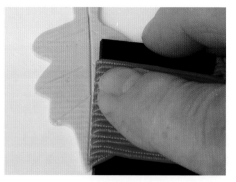

3 Try making a stamp with an all-over texture, such as a leaf. Cut out the shape with a cutter, mark the veins with a blade and then press a texture paddle (see page 55) or similar tool across the whole leaf. Press the leaf onto the glass as before, but don't press too hard or you will lose the texture.

4 Fold the leftover sheet of clay in half to double the thickness to 1/4in (6mm). Cut out a piece big enough to cover each of the stamp designs and press them on top of the shapes. Place the glass onto a piece of cardstock or cardboard and bake.

Inking the stamps

Bring the ink pad to the stamp and tap, tap, tap on the stamp until it looks shiny. Don't rub the ink pad over the stamp or it may get overloaded with ink.

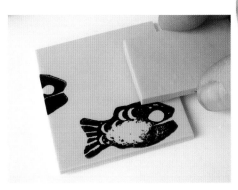

Using stamps

1 Holding the edges of the stamp, load it with ink and then press it gently onto the clay. You can see here that the head and tail have printed fairly well, but the body has not. This type of printed effect can be suitable for pieces that you want to look aged or distressed.

2 A more reliable way of achieving a complete, detailed print is to press the clay onto the stamp. This can be more difficult in terms of positioning, but the resulting print is more complete.

3 You can use stamps to create a printed texture rather than for printing images or patterns. Use a combination of pressing the stamp onto the clay and vice versa to get different effects. Placing a thin piece of packing foam under the clay when printing onto it can help achieve better coverage.

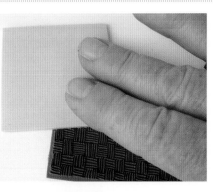

Rubber sheet stamps

1 Unmounted rubber sheet stamps can be used to print onto flat sheets of clay in the usual way, but because they are flexible they can also be wrapped around clay shapes such as beads and vessels. This takes practice and it is harder to get a clean print, but it can allow you to create printing effects that would otherwise be difficult to achieve.

2 When using rubber stamps, only press lightly unless you want to texture the clay at the same time. The wet ink will act as a resist so that the stamp does not stick to the clay, but do not leave the clay on the stamp too long or the ink will dry and the clay might tear when you try to remove it.

Shell bead
Marie Segal

Two flat sheets of champagne clay are printed with a symmetrical shell design. Once the ink is dry, the shapes are cut out using a craft knife, holding the blade so that the edge is angled in toward the back of the clay sheet. The two shell shapes are then placed together and the edge seams very carefully pinched together. This takes practice but can be done because the ink dries permanently. Small balls of black clay are added on either side of the base of the shell and then pierced through. After baking, the shell bead is colored with alcohol ink or fabric markers, letting the ink on one side dry before coloring the other (you can use a heat gun to speed things up), and then the finished bead is rebaked.

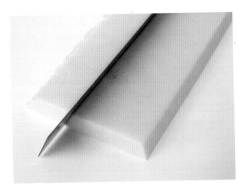

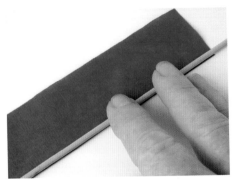

Ink-printed tube beads

1 Roll out the clay, ⅛in (3mm) thick, and fold in half to double the thickness. Trim the sheet to about 1½ x 3in (4 x 7.5cm). Use a tissue blade to cut along the length of the clay, angling the blade outward from the center. Repeat on the other side to create a trapezoid shape in cross section. The top of the sheet should be ¾–1in (2–2.5cm) wide for a ⁵⁄₃₂in (2mm) thick skewer.

2 Cut a strip of masking tape about 4in (10cm) long. Press a bamboo skewer onto the very edge of the tape and then roll up the tape and the skewer tightly together. Roll forward and backward to make sure that the closing edge of the tape is stuck down.

3 Place the skewer along the center of the clay sheet and bring both sides of the clay together, matching the beveled edges. Pinch the edges together and use a fingertip to smooth the clay until there is no visible join. Roll the clay on your work surface until it is smooth and even along the whole length.

4 Take hold of the whole length of the clay in one hand and twist it to loosen it from the skewer. Once loosened, roll the clay again to smooth any marks from its surface. To trim the clay to the required length of bead, place the tissue blade across one end of the clay and then roll the bead forward to cut through the clay. Pull off the excess clay, then measure the required length along the skewer and repeat.

5 Tap the ink pad onto the stamp until it is completely coated. When the stamp is inked well, the pattern will look shiny and solid. You will only get one chance to ink the bead, so take the time to ink the stamp well.

6 Place a sheet of thin foam under the stamp to cushion it. Place the skewered bead at the edge of the stamp and carefully roll forward until the whole bead has been printed with the inked pattern. Try to avoid rolling too far or an area of the bead will be double-printed with ink. For extra precision, measure the circumference of the bead to see how far you will have to roll it on the stamp.

Ink-printed beads

Ink-printed bead

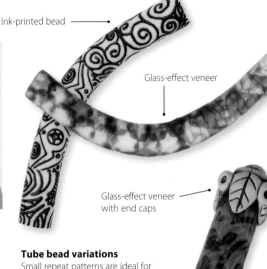

Glass-effect veneer

Glass-effect veneer with end caps

7 Press the point of the skewer into a ball of scrap clay stuck to the work surface and leave until the ink dries. To test if the ink is dry, lightly touch the bead with a finger. Do not rub your finger across it. If no ink comes off, the bead is dry enough to continue. Trim the ends as before.

8 Gently pull the bead off the skewer. By holding the ends of the bead, you can bend it into a curved shape. Check the bead carefully to see if the ink has double-printed on any part of it. If it has, position the double-printed section on the inside curve or the back of the bead.

Tube bead variations
Small repeat patterns are ideal for printing onto tube beads. Also try laminating a veneer of glass-effect clay (see page 68) around a plain tube bead. Decorative end caps also look good.

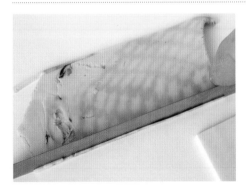

Using ink scraps
1 You can create interesting effects using leftover ink-printed scraps such as from making tube beads. Roll out the scrap clay, then fold in half with the ink on the inside and roll again. Repeat once more. Carefully cut tiny slivers—1/32in (1mm) or less—off the edge of the printed sheet, sliding the blade toward you so that the slivers stick to the blade.

2 Place the slivers, one at a time, onto a plain sheet of clay. Start at one edge and work your way to the opposite edge, placing each new sliver touching the previous one. Continue until the background sheet is full or you run out of ink scraps.

3 Roll over the slivers to tack everything together. Start by rolling in the direction of the slivers, then turn the sheet 90 degrees and roll across them. Do not press very hard, but just enough to set the slivers in place. Trim the edges and bake. You can use the same technique with other patterned sheets of clay (see page 85).

PRINTING EFFECTS

Glass effects

Translucent clay gives the look of frosted glass after baking or, if handled properly, aged glass. When thin sheets of ink-printed translucent clay are layered together, the result is reminiscent of the caned patterns of Murano glass, without the amount of work or extreme heat involved. As well as printing ink patterns onto the clay, you can add other materials such as glitter and metal leaf between the layers. You do not have to limit yourself to ink either; mica powder with alcohol ink produces a lovely effect.

You will need:

- Translucent and champagne clay
- Pasta machine, roller and tissue blade
- Rubber sheet stamp
- Solvent-based ink pads in several colors (red and black are used here; a good three-color combination is blue, lime green and purple; add black and magenta for a five-color combination)
- Metallic acrylic paint (bronze and gold acrylic paint are used here) or metallic ink pad (such as Brilliance)
- Small paintbrush if using paint

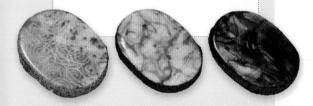

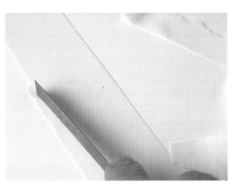

1 Roll out some translucent clay as thinly as you can. The clay shown here is less than 1/64in (0.5mm) thick, but if you have trouble rolling such thin sheets, roll them a little thicker—1/32in (1mm) would be fine. Cut out two strips the same size and then a third strip that is the same width but half the length of the first two.

2 Tap the red ink pad onto a rubber stamp until the stamp is shiny with ink. Tapping rather than rubbing the pad onto the stamp will prevent the stamp from getting overloaded with ink. Turning the ink pad upside down so that the lid rests on your work surface will make it easy to lift out and replace the ink pad during use.

3 Lay a long strip of translucent clay onto the inked stamp, lightly pressing it down to pick up the ink. The idea is to print the ink pattern onto the clay, not impress the pattern.

Glitter disk beads
Cover both sides of a 1/4in (6mm) thick sheet of light-colored clay with a veneer of glass-effect clay and then cut out. After baking, glue glitter around the edges.

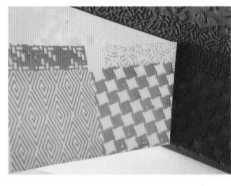

4 Carefully peel the clay off the stamp to reveal the printed design. Do this immediately after pressing the clay onto the stamp, because once the ink begins to dry, the very thin clay may stick to the stamp and tear as you try to remove it. Set the strip aside to let the ink dry completely (about 10 minutes).

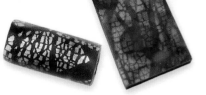

Gold crackle glass
Apply a sheet of gold leaf to the base clay and roll to create a crackle effect, then add a veneer of glass-effect clay.

5 Clean any remaining wet red ink off the stamp (a baby wipe or alcohol wipe is useful for this), then ink up another area of the stamp with black ink. Lay the second long strip of translucent clay onto the inked area and press down lightly. Peel the clay carefully off the stamp and allow to dry.

6 Apply some metallic acrylic paint to the shorter strip of translucent clay—here, diagonal bronze stripes crossed by gold stripes, but you can paint them any way you choose. Alternatively, stamp with a metallic ink. Allow the paint to dry.

7 Once all three strips are completely dry, lay the red strip over the black one, both with inked sides uppermost. Press them gently together. By using an ink that dries completely on the clay, you can touch the inked surface without marring it. It also means that you will not get ink all over your hands and your tools when you work with it.

Glass-effect bangle and ring
Marie Segal

Laminated layers of translucent clay printed in blue, purple and black are wrapped around a log of white clay. A small amount of PVA or Ultimate glue is applied to the channel around a brass bracelet blank and left until tacky. The clay is then wrapped around the blank, with the seam on the inside against the glue. Once the clay feels securely in the channel, it is smoothed into shape. Leftover scraps are rolled into a ball and then shaped into a ring. Both pieces are then baked, quenched and sanded.

8 Lay the metallic strip on top of the left side of the two inked strips. Here, it is placed paint side down, but it does not matter. Fold the right side of the layered strips over the left side and press together. Use a roller to tack the layers firmly together. Lift the strip free from the work surface; if it has stuck, slide a tissue blade under it.

9 If you wish, you can roll the laminated strips more thinly at this point, turning the piece 90 degrees each time you roll so that the design spreads out evenly. Roll out a sheet of champagne clay, ⅛in (3mm) thick. Lay the laminated strips over the clay sheet. Press down gently and then use a roller to tack them together well. Trim the excess printed strip, then bake and quench.

PRINTING EFFECTS

Screen printing

Screen printing is a quick and easy way to print a pattern or image onto polymer clay. Ready-made silk screen designs are widely available or you can buy a kit to make your own. There are also plenty of alternative materials to traditional silk screen that will produce good results, from lace fabric to window screen mesh.

You will need:

- Polymer clay and roller
- Screen material, such as traditional silk screen, window screen mesh, plastic tablecloth with cutout pattern or lace fabric
- Silk screen or acrylic fabric paint and paintbrushes
- Silk screen squeegee or improvised tool, such as a piece of cardstock, cardboard, chipboard, an old credit card or a popsicle stick
- Brass stencil and stencil brush

Dagger earrings
Lynda Braunstein-Gilcher
A silk screen is used to print a pattern onto clay using acrylic paint, and then shapes are cut out to make earrings with sterling silver findings.

One-color printing
1 Plastic window mesh is used as a screen here, but the same technique can be applied for any type of screen material. Lay the screen over the clay and press it down with your fingers to set it in place. Gently roll across it with a roller to make sure that it is flat and lightly adhered to the clay.

3 Drag the paint across the screen with a squeegee or improvised scraper (here, a piece of chipboard). Lay the scraper almost flat and drag from bottom to top. Turn over the scraper and drag from top to bottom. If necessary, drag from corner to corner. The aim is to spread out the paint very thinly in a nice, even layer that completely covers the clay.

2 Use a paintbrush to apply some paint along the bottom of the clay over the screen. A fluid acrylic fabric paint is being used here, but if you are using a tube of thick paint, simply squeeze a bead of paint along the bottom of the clay.

Line caused by stopping partway when peeling off the screen.

4 Carefully peel away the screen from the clay in one fluid motion. If you hesitate or stop partway, you may get a line across the clay at that point; this happened when stopping to take this picture (see inset). Allow the paint to dry completely overnight and then bake.

Two-color printing

1 A plastic tablecloth with a cutout pattern is used as a screen here. Place the tablecloth face down on the clay with the flat back of the cloth uppermost. Press down with your fingers and then roll across it with a roller. Use paintbrushes to apply different colors of paint to different areas (here, red russet at the bottom and pearl at the top).

2 Spread the paint evenly over the cloth; an index card folded in half is used as an improvised scraper here. Carefully peel off the cloth, allow to dry and then bake.

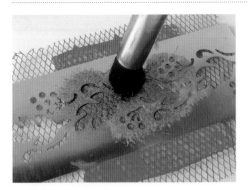

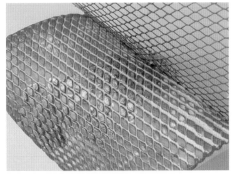

Screen and stencil

1 Lay the screen (this one is copper craft mesh) over the clay and spread a layer of paint across the whole surface, as before. Allow the paint to dry slightly and then place a stencil on top, holding it in place with one hand. Apply paint by dabbing a stencil brush in an up-and-down motion onto the stencil. Apply a second coat if necessary.

2 Gently lift off the stencil and then allow the paint to dry before removing the wire screen. When using a fairly rigid screen such as this, you may have to peel the clay from the screen rather than the other way around. Do this carefully, starting at one corner and working to the other side, and then carefully flatten the clay with your fingers.

Tips & techniques

- If you are using traditional silk screen, it is best to use silk screen paint. This smooth, creamy paint is perfect for penetrating the fine silk mesh.

- Light-bodied acrylic fabric paints that are permanent when heat-set work well for screen printing. When applied to raw clay, allowed to dry completely and then baked, the printed pattern will be set on the clay. To be sure of the paint sticking when applied to baked clay, put the printed clay back into the oven at 200°F (95°C) for 15 minutes and then allow to cool.

- Take care when using a fluid acrylic paint that you do not apply too much or you may find the pattern marred when you lift the screen. Paste-like or viscous acrylic is easier to spread evenly.

- Avoid paint that contains particles because these may plug the screen or be dragged across the clay and mark it.

- A silk screen squeegee is ideal for spreading the paint, but there are plenty of good alternatives that you probably already have in your tool box if you want to experiment—cardboard, chipboard, an old credit card or even a popsicle stick.

- To remove any texture left by the screen, let the paint dry and then roll out the clay to flatten the sheet a little. Turn the sheet 90 degrees and roll again, slightly more thinly (the next setting on a pasta machine). Rotate and roll twice more. This will stretch the clay and its printed design evenly in all directions. The clay will be very thin afterward, perfect for using as a veneer or as a backing on a brooch.

- Try using cutters to cut out different shapes from screen-printed clay and use them to decorate other items.

PRINTING EFFECTS

Image transfer

There are numerous types of image transfer papers available; waterslide transfers are quick and simple to use. You can also use liquid clay to transfer images. You can transfer your own printed images or use ones cut out of catalogs, magazines or other printed media (but take care about copyright). There are so many variables when working with image transfer that you just have to try it with the tools and materials you have in order to find out what results you will get.

You will need:

- Polymer clay on which to transfer the images (white or a light color is best; stronger colors will show through)
- Scissors
- For waterslide transfer:
  » Waterslide transfer paper (paper with pre-printed images is used here, but printable paper is also available for transferring your own images)
  » Shallow bowl or plate with a little water in it
  » Towel
- For liquid clay transfer:
  » Liquid clay
  » Images printed onto glossy paper (make sure that the ink is dry)
  » Sheet of glass (such as from a picture frame)
  » Toothpick or piece of cardboard, chipboard or popsicle stick
  » Container in which to soak images, such as a glass tumbler

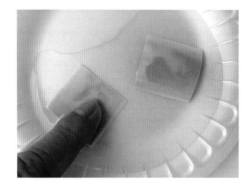

Waterslide transfer

1 Cut out the images on the transfer paper that you wish to use (transfers can be cut after they are on the clay, but it is not as easy). Place the images face down in a little water for a minute or so; they tend to curl up, so press them flat until they stay that way. When the transfer is ready to use, it will slide easily off the backing paper.

Collage heart necklace
Tejae Floyde
A polymer clay heart is embellished with a collage of digital images, transferred using the artist's own transfer paper, and then strung on a beaded chain.

2 Place the edge of the image onto a sheet of clay and slide the rest of the backing paper from the transfer. Hold the transfer in place with one finger and slide another finger gently across the surface to press out the water from one side of the image to the other.

3 Daub any remaining water from the surface with a towel (or a paper towel). When the image is completely dry, you can apply a very thin layer of liquid clay over it to protect it and then bake. Alternatively, coat it with a layer of varnish or glaze after baking. If you apply the image to a very thin layer of clay, you can suspend it in a layer of resin.

Glass is an ideal baking surface. You can check for bubbles, the baked image will be easy to peel off and the glass will give it a smooth surface. A ceramic tile is a good alternative.

Liquid clay transfer

1 Cut away any extra paper from around the image and then apply liquid clay over the top. Make sure that the whole image is covered. You can use a toothpick to spread the clay around on small images; for larger ones, use a piece of stiff cardboard, chipboard or a popsicle stick to spread the liquid clay. A layer at least ¹⁄₃₂in (1mm) thick is a good amount to work with.

2 Press the image face down onto a sheet of glass. The liquid clay should flow to the outside edges of the image. If necessary, press on it just a little to make sure that this happens. Turn the glass over to double-check this and to make sure that there are no air bubbles. You can trim away any excess liquid clay with scissors after baking.

3 Look through the glass to check for air bubbles. If there are any, press them to the outside of the image or peel the piece off the glass and add more liquid clay. Place the image back in the same place afterward. Bake the liquid clay in the usual way and peel off the glass when cool. If necessary, use the edge of a tissue blade to scrape the image from the glass.

4 Submerge the baked pieces in some water and soak for about 30 minutes. Take the pieces out of the water and rub off the paper from the back. If the paper remains stuck on the back of the liquid clay, return the piece to the water and soak for longer.

5 Spread some liquid clay over the polymer clay onto which the image is to be transferred. Lay the liquid clay image on top and rub a finger across it to squeeze out any air bubbles between the image and the clay below. Spread more liquid clay on top, then bake and allow to cool. Use scissors to trim away any excess image.

Collage business card case
Lisa Pavelka

This mixed media piece includes waterslide image transfer, Sutton slice, stamping, crackling, metal leafing and millefiori accents. Metal components are embedded into the clay.

PRINTING EFFECTS

Tile samples

Printing is a versatile way of creating decorative effects with polymer clay, from printing with commercial and homemade stamps to laminating layers of printed translucent clay to create the entirely different look of decorative colored glass. You can use traditional silk screen printing techniques with polymer clay, as well as apply color to printed designs using permanent markers, colored pencils, oil paints, acrylics and inks. The surface of polymer clay makes an excellent canvas for many mediums.

Glass-effect bangles

Marie Segal

Layers of ink-printed translucent clay are laminated onto a base of non-printed clay in various colors (rainbow blend, white and purple). The clay is then wrapped around brass blanks to make bangles (see page 69).

PEN AND INK

1 Paisley

Black ink pad and colored pigment pens; white clay

How-to: Use rubber stamps to print an outline design onto the clay in black ink (see page 65). Bake the piece to heat-set the ink and cure the clay. Color the design using pigment pens, then put back into the oven for a short time to set the pigment pen ink.

2 Window blinds

Black ink pad and colored markers; black and white clay

How-to: Make a sheet of clay in alternating black and white stripes (see page 86). Stamp an outline design in black ink (see page 65), then bake to heat-set the ink. Color the design using marker pens, then bake again for a short time to set the marker ink.

3 Flaming love

Fine-point Lumocolor pens; white clay

How-to: Draw a design onto baked clay. The color will remain strong and will not rub off. If you need to rebake the clay for any reason, there will be very little change in the color. This is not the case with some pens, so experiment before embarking on an important piece. Use a fine-point pen to personalize clay pieces with your signature.

INK STAMPING

4 Carp pond
Black ink pad; champagne clay
How-to: Use a variety of rubber stamps to print a design onto the clay (see page 65). Overlapping the prints and combining pictorial and textural patterns can be very effective. Allow the ink to dry and then bake.

7 Zooplankton
Black ink pad and glitter embossing powder; baked white clay tile
How-to: Apply ink to a rubber sheet stamp and then use the stamp to print onto the white tile (see page 65). Sprinkle embossing powder over the wet ink, let it sit for a few moments and then shake off the excess powder. Blow on the tile to remove excess but do not touch. Bake and allow to cool before touching.

5 Follow me
Black ink pad; champagne clay
How-to: Make your own stamp using polymer clay (see page 64). Make the stamp bold in outline with strongly defined details. To print with it, try pressing the stamp onto polymer clay and vice versa, then compare the results (see page 65).

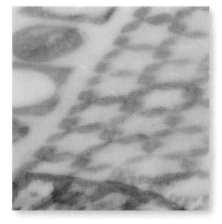

INK SCRAPS

8 Waste not, want not
Black ink pad; flesh-colored clay
How-to: Roll out the clay, stamp a design onto it and let the ink dry (or use leftover ink-printed scraps such as from making beads; see page 67). Fold the clay in half with the ink on the inside and roll out. Repeat once or twice more, then bake.

6 Printed leaf texture
Green ink pad; champagne clay
How-to: Make your own stamp using polymer clay, giving the stamp a more subtle all-over texture than the fish stamp used for tile 5 (see page 64). To print with it, overlap the prints to create a printed texture rather than a defined pattern or image (see page 65).

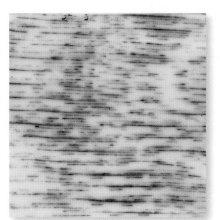

9 Fuzzy stripes
Black ink pad; flesh-colored clay
How-to: Instead of baking tile 8, cut thin slivers from the edge and place them onto a sheet of plain clay, positioning the slivers close together (see page 67). Use a roller to attach the slivers to the plain sheet, then bake.

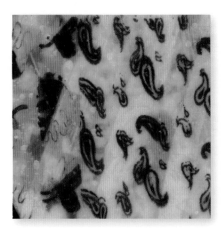

GLASS EFFECTS

10 Floating feathers

Ink pads and metallic acrylic paint; translucent and champagne clay

How-to: Print very thin strips of translucent clay with red and black ink designs. Paint metallic acrylic onto another strip. Allow to dry, then sandwich together, roll out and apply to a sheet of champagne clay (see page 68). Bake and quench.

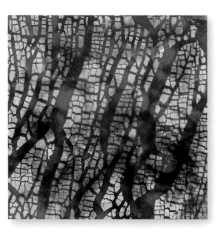

13 Sea glass

Ink pads and gold leaf; translucent and brown clay

How-to: Roll out the brown clay and apply a sheet of gold leaf (see page 34). Roll the clay again, then turn 90 degrees and roll once more to create a crackle effect. Apply three or four thin layers of ink-stamped translucent on top, roll together, then bake and quench (see page 68).

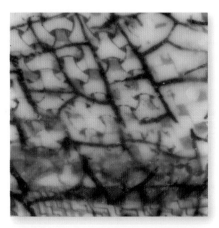

11 Distant shores

Ink pads; translucent and white clay

How-to: This is made in the same way as tile 10 but using different colors. Here, there are three layers: the bottom layer is purple, the second layer blue and the top layer black.

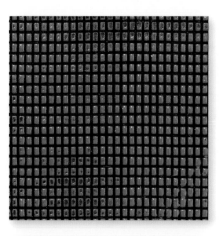

SCREEN PRINTING

14 Gridlock

Red acrylic paint; black clay

How-to: Lay plastic window screen mesh over a sheet of clay. Apply paint and spread evenly. Peel off screen, allow paint to dry, then bake (see page 70).

12 Amethyst glitter

Ink pad and glitter slivers; translucent and violet clay

How-to: Use a rubber stamp and black ink to print a design onto a thin sheet of translucent and allow to dry (see page 68). Roll out a thicker sheet of violet clay, sprinkle on some glitter slivers and then lay the printed translucent sheet ink side down on top. Roll together, then bake and quench.

15 Golden geisha

Ocher acrylic paint; black clay

How-to: This is made in the same way as tile 14, but using silk screen. You can buy ready-made silk screen designs or make your own (follow the instructions on the pack).

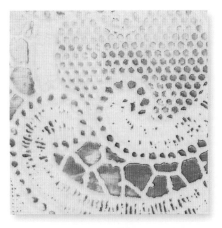

16 Barnacles

Red russet and pearl acrylic paint; white clay

How-to: Lay plastic tablecloth with cutout pattern textured side down onto a sheet of clay. Apply red paint along bottom of clay and pearl paint along top. Spread the paint evenly, then peel off cloth. Allow to dry and then bake (see page 71).

IMAGE TRANSFER

19 Waterfall

Liquid clay and white clay

How-to: Apply liquid clay over front of photograph, place image side down onto sheet of glass and bake. Soak in water, then rub off the paper backing. Spread some liquid clay onto a sheet of white clay, then apply the image, spread more liquid clay on top and bake (see page 73).

17 Lace flowers

Gold acrylic paint; black clay

How-to: This is made in the same way as tile 14, but using lace fabric as the screen material. This fabric has a flower design but there are numerous lace patterns available.

20 Lovers' kiss

White clay

How-to: Immerse a waterslide transfer in some water for a minute or so, then place it onto a sheet of white clay and slide the backing paper from the transfer (see page 72). You can apply a protective coat of liquid clay and then bake, or coat with varnish, glaze or resin after baking.

18 Stenciled grid

Red and light blue metallic acrylic paint; white clay

How-to: Screen print with red acrylic using copper craft mesh. Place leaf stencil on top and apply blue acrylic through the stencil shapes (see page 71). Allow to dry and then bake.

21 Framed geisha

Liquid clay and green clay (yellow, green, pearl white and gold mixture)

How-to: Transfer a waterslide image onto the clay in the same way as tile 20. This image has a printed border, so the surrounding clay looks like a picture frame. Apply a protective coat of liquid clay and then bake.

PRINTING EFFECTS

Polymer clay
artists at work

The beautiful pieces displayed here show how artists combine printing effects with a multitude of other techniques to give a bold and dynamic statement to their art pieces. From combining silk-screen printing with texturing effects to setting an image transfer against a glowing foil background, the artists bring together different techniques to create imaginative and harmonious designs.

» See pages 74–77 for tile samples

Graffiti leaves necklace
Lynda Braunstein-Gilcher

Techniques used: The smaller leaves at the front are silk screened with acrylic paint, while the larger leaves at the back are textured with radiating lines. The different-colored clay leaves are tied together by the use a single color of acrylic paint to create a cohesive unit. The leaves are threaded together with small seed beads in a harmonious color. The larger leaves are about 1¼in (3cm) long.
See SCREEN PRINTING tiles 14–15

► Happy feet box
Helen Wyland-Malchow

Techniques used: The 7½in (19cm) diameter hollow-form sphere has been sanded to 60 grit so that the lines from sanding are still visible. The 8½in (21.5cm) diameter top collar is made from white polymer clay, with the design drawn in graphite, colored pencils and marker pens. Sanding polymer clay with 80- or 100-grit paper makes it easier to apply drawn designs; it works best with colored pencils. Nickel silver wire with vintage plastic balls are added to the base of the bowl, and black onyx cabochons are attached to the top for extra decoration.
See PEN AND INK tiles 1–3

▼ Hollow beads
Debbie Crothers

Techniques used: These hollow-core beads are embellished with a veneer made from raw clay colored with alcohol inks and then decorated with stamped images using StazOn ink, glitter, foils, gold leaf and mica powders. The beads are coated with liquid clay for a glossy finish and measure about 1¾in (4.5cm) diameter.
See PEN AND INK tile 1, INK STAMPING tile 4 and GLASS EFFECTS tile 12

► Madonna and child electric pendant

Nancy Ulrich

Techniques used: This 2¾ x 1⅝in (7 x 4cm) pendant captures the look of an old stained-glass window. The textured foil behind the waterslide image transfer gives the impression of light shining through a pane of old glass, lighting up the picture of mother and child like a stained-glass cathedral window. The foil and image decoration is covered with clear resin. The pendant is hung from a string of foil-covered and plain black tube beads, tying the whole thing together visually. The piece is framed with a simple but effective border of black clay.

See IMAGE TRANSFER tiles 20–21

▼ Votive candle shade

Marie Segal

Techniques used: This simple but effective design is made from four sheets of clay in blended rainbow colors. A rubber stamp is used to print a bamboo design in ink on each panel. The same effect could be created using screen printing. Each baked panel is glued to a pair of popsicle sticks, painted with black acrylic. Holes are drilled through the sticks and the panels are connected using black-coated copper wire. Cernit clay is used to make the panels because of its porcelain effect. When a small candle in a glass holder is placed inside the shade, the light shows through the panels. The candle shade stands about 4½in (11.5cm) high and is about 3½in (9cm) square.

See INK STAMPING tiles 4–5

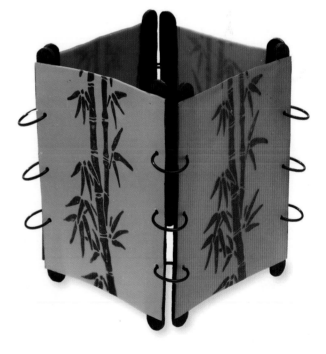

◄ Lady in blue bangle

Alice Stroppel

Techniques used: A brass bracelet blank is covered with polymer clay and a design is drawn onto the clay with pen and ink and alcohol inks. The bracelet is shown from six different angles so that you can see the whole of the design. The bracelet is 1¼in (3cm) wide.

See PEN AND INK tiles 1–3

CANING & STACKING

Basic canework

Canework follows the same principles as millefiori glassmaking, in which rods of colored glass are fused and stretched to create a glass cane with a pattern running through it. Similarly, different colors and shapes of polymer clay can be combined to create canes. Slices of the cane can be used as they are, or the cane can be reduced and stretched so that the pattern inside is miniaturized. Simple canes, such as bull's-eyes and spirals, can be combined to build complex canes.

You will need:

- Pasta machine, roller, tissue blade and ripple blade
- Polymer clay in translucent, white, black and a variety of colors—use whatever color combinations you like; refer to step-by-step instructions and photographs if you want to replicate the colors shown
  - Bamboo skewer and transfer foil for confetti dots (overleaf)

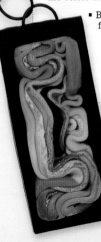

Distorted cane pendant
Marie Segal
After reducing the cane on page 86, the distorted ends are sliced off and added to a sheet of black clay textured with sandpaper to form a pendant.

Rainbow spiral cane
1 Mix a sheet of translucent rainbow colors (see page 22 and use the strip arrangement for blended colors), then roll it into a long strip (see page 23). Roll out some white clay, ⅟₆₄in (0.5mm) thick. Place the rainbow strip on top of the white clay, then trim the edges to match but leave the front edge of the white clay ¼in (6mm) longer. Fold the front edge over and tuck it in tightly.

2 Roll up the two sheets together like a cinnamon roll, making it as tight as possible. You can vary the thickness and number of layers in the spiral cane if you wish.

3 Press in the sides of the cane to form a waist at the center. Rotate the cane slightly and press again. Continue all around the cane, then gradually work outward to each end, pressing and rotating as you go. Continue until the cane is reduced to half its original diameter. Roll the cane to smooth it out, then trim off the distorted ends.

4 Use a tissue blade to cut slices from the cane. Try cutting some straight and some diagonally. If you are using very soft clay and want to cut very thin slices, you may have to let the cane rest to allow the clay to firm up. This may take an hour or a couple of days, depending on the consistency of the clay.

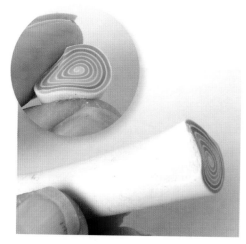

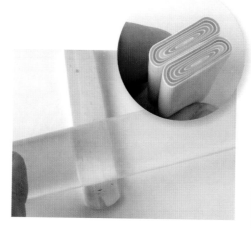

5 You can reshape the cane using a similar process to reduction, but this time just pinch the cane to form the shape you want rather than squeezing or pressing it. The idea is to reshape it, not stretch it any further. Here, the round spiral cane is pinched along one edge to form a teardrop shape.

6 Take a 3in (7.5cm) section of the rainbow cane and use a roller to flatten it a little. Peel the cane off the work surface every now and again to keep it from sticking and allow it to lengthen to about 4in (10cm). Cut the cane in half and stack one half on top of the other, with cut edges together. Press together so that they will not come apart.

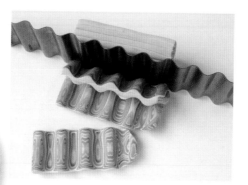

7 Flatten the cane once again and lengthen to about 4in (10cm). Cut the cane in half and stack together, as before. Cut and stack a third time so that you have eight layers of the flattened spiral cane pattern. Press the layers together.

8 Stand the cane stack on edge and use a ripple blade to cut off a slice, just over ⅛in (3mm) thick. The distorted blade will cut through the many layers of the spirals. For subsequent slices, align the ripples of the blade with the ripples of the previous cut. Lay several slices side by side and roll flat to create a single patterned sheet.

Reducing the cane

This involves reducing the thickness of the cane by means of compressing and lengthening it. Work gradually, reducing the cane a little at a time to keep distortion to a minimum. There are various reduction methods, but start by trying the following:

▪ Round cane: Squeeze the cane all along its length, starting at the center and working outward, and rotating the cane as you work. You can roll the reduced cane on your work surface like a log to smooth out fingermarks.

▪ Triangle cane: Place the cane on your work surface. Starting at the center and working outward, pinch along the top angle of the triangle and press down onto the work surface at the same time so that the cane begins to lengthen. Turn the cane onto its next side and repeat this process until the cane is the size you require.

▪ Square or rectangular cane: Place the cane on your work surface. Starting at the center and working outward, press down along the top of the cane. Turn the cane onto its next side and repeat until the cane is the size you require. You can also squeeze along opposite sides of the cane to reduce it. Every now and again, pinch along the corners to maintain sharp angles. You can use a roller to smooth the surfaces.

▪ Irregular-shaped canes: Do not press or squeeze canes that have indentations or an irregular shape. Instead, hold the ends and very carefully pull them.

▪ Distorted ends: The ends of canes become distorted during reduction. Cut them off when you have finished (trimming the ends earlier would just create a new end to become distorted). These ends can be used as scrap clay or even as a decorative embellishment.

Insert colors as shown so that there will be plain pearl sections between the colors after mixing.

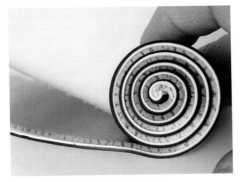

Faux shell cane

1 Mix a sheet of pearlized colors, using pearl clay as the base clay with strips of blue, magenta, violet and purple inserted as shown, then roll the clay into a long strip (see pages 22–23).

2 Roll out long strips of white and black clay, each ⅟₆₄in (0.5mm) thick. Layer the three strips with black at the bottom, then white and finally the colored strip on top. Trim the edges of the strips, roll up into a spiral cane and reduce to half its original diameter (see page 81). You can use the spiral cane as it is or continue to create a basketweave-patterned stack.

End-of-the-cane pendant
Marie Segal

The end of the faux shell spiral cane is sliced off before the cane is reduced. The slice is applied to a textured clay pendant.

3 Flatten the spiral cane into a rectangular shape, then cut in half and stack. Press the two halves together to create a square cross section. Cut in half and stack together, but this time rotate one of the halves 90 degrees. Cut in half and stack together once more, rotating one half to continue the basketweave pattern.

4 Press the whole thing together, then flatten into a rectanglular shape. Cut in half and stack so that the basketweave pattern continues.

5 Use a ripple blade to cut slices from the side of the stack. Roll the slices through the pasta machine on the thickest setting, passing the ripples vertically through the machine to maintain the design, or horizontally if you want to spread the design. Both sides of the slice will be slightly different from each other, and each slice will be different from the next.

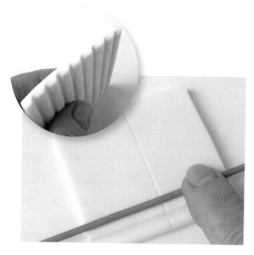

Confetti dots

1 Roll out some translucent clay, ⅛in (3mm) thick, then fold in half to double the thickness. Trim to about 2¼in (6cm) square. Use a tissue blade to mark the halfway point (do not cut through). Use a skewer to press channels across the clay every ¼in (6mm) or so. The channels should cross the halfway mark.

2 Roll out several logs of clay, 3⁄32in (2mm) thick, and lightly press them into the channels up to the halfway mark. Take care not to press them out of their circular shape. A rainbow of different colors is used here, but you can use any colors you like or just a single color.

3 Cut the sheet at the halfway mark and lightly place the cut section over the logs, aligning the ends neatly. Trim the logs at the other end. Check that everything is lined up correctly, then press the sheets together to sandwich the logs inside.

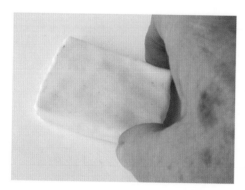

Try applying slivers to a foil-covered sheet of clay. The foil will show through after baking (see tile 14, page 96).

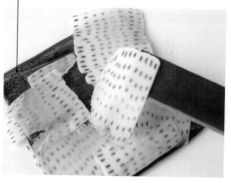

4 Reduce the whole piece, pressing inward along the side edges so that it lengthens in the direction that the logs lie. Lengthen to about 6in (15cm), taking care to maintain square corners by pinching them into shape now and again. You can use a roller to lengthen the cane, but do not use too much force because the aim is to keep the logs inside as round as possible.

5 Cut in half and stack one half on top of the other, cut edges together. Here, dots of the same color are aligned, but you could flip one half if you wish. Roll gently with a roller to tack them together. Reduce and lengthen the stack as before, to about 5in (12.5cm), then cut in half and stack again.

6 Repeat this lengthening, halving and stacking process twice more, until you have 16 layers in the stack. You can cut off ⅛in (3mm) thick slices from the block and lay them side by side; lightly roll to tack them together to form a larger sheet. Another option is to slice off thin slivers and apply them as a veneer in overlapping layers.

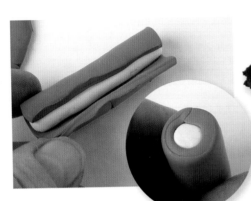

Bull's-eye canes

1 Roll a log of white clay and a sheet of blue clay. Lay the log across the front edge of the sheet. Trim the edge straight and trim the width to match the length of the log. Roll up until the front edge touches and marks the sheet. Trim along the mark and then butt the edges together around the log.

2 Roll out a sheet of black clay and wrap the bull's-eye inside the black clay as before. You can vary the number of layers in the bull's-eye cane and the thickness of each layer. This cane consists of a white log wrapped in a thick sheet of blue clay and then a slightly thinner sheet of black clay. Reduce the cane to the required thickness (see page 81).

3 You can reshape a round bull's-eye into a triangle or square by pinching along the cane to form the angles. Alternatively, reshape the original log into a triangle or square and then wrap it, maintaining the shape by pinching along the angles. When reducing the log, take care to maintain the angles.

African trade tile

1 Make a round and triangular bull's-eye cane (see above). Reduce both to ¼in (6mm) thick. Cut the round cane into thirds and tack them together side by side so that you can apply slices of three bull's-eyes at a time. Cut the triangle cane into quarters and tack side by side, inverting alternate ones. Cut one of the end quarters in half and transfer the cut half to the other side, so that you have a straight-edged strip of triangles. Apply four rows of alternating cane slices along the center of a 2in (5cm) square sheet of blue clay.

2 Roll thin logs of yellow and black clay. Twist them together at one end and hold that end while you use another finger to roll the other end so that the two colors twist together. Place a length of twisted log above and below the rows of cane slices, pressing them into place.

3 Roll a thin log of gold clay and place a length on either side of the twisted logs. Tack them into place by pressing gently. Roll with a roller in the direction of the logs and cane rows. This will flatten the canes and logs into the background sheet of clay to firmly attach them. Trim the edges.

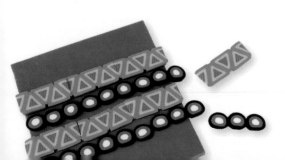

The cane consists of a translucent gold log wrapped in a thin sheet of white, a thicker sheet of translucent blue and another thin sheet of white.

Window cane

1 Make a 1½in (4cm) long bull's-eye cane, pinching along the angles to shape it into a square and reducing until it is about 4in (10cm) long (see opposite and page 81). Cut in half and put the two halves side by side, cut edges together. Cut in half again and stack to form a block of four squares.

2 Reduce the cane as before, pressing along each side of the square from the center outward until the cane is about 4in (10cm) long again. Cut in half and stack together. Lengthen once again to about 4in (10cm), then cut in half and stack to form a block of 16 squares.

3 Cut thin slices from the window cane and place them side by side on a sheet of clay (champagne clay is used here), maintaining the pattern of squares. Lightly roll with a roller to attach the cane slices to the background sheet. Trim any overlap at the edges, then bake and quench to enhance the translucency.

Zigzag stripes

1 Make a three-color blend of black, white and brown clay (see page 130). Cut off a 1in (2.5cm) section, flip it so that the colors are swapped around and then stack it on the end of the blended strip. Cut off the two-layer section and place on the end of the blended strip so that the colors begin to form a zigzag pattern.

2 Continue cutting and stacking sections to create a zigzag of alternating colors.

Bargello tile on canvas *Leila Bidler*
Thin slivers cut from a complex cane of blended stripes are offset and applied to canvas to create a zigzagging stripe pattern in the style of bargello embroidery.

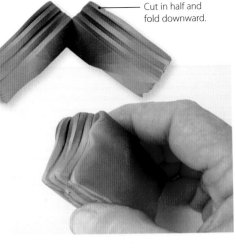

Make a template for cutting out the triangles of clay when mixing the color blend (see page 21).

Cut in half and fold downward.

"Between the spaces" complex cane

1 Make a Skinner blend of red, blue and yellow clay (see page 20). Straighten the edge and cut off a 1–1½in (2.5–4cm) section. Rotate it so that the colors are swapped around, and then stack it on the end of the blended sheet. Continue cutting, rotating and stacking until you have six layers of alternating colors.

2 Cut the stack in half and fold the two halves down against each other. With your fingers against the cut edge and your thumb against the opposite edge, compress the stack together and begin lengthening it to front and back. What you are doing here is changing the orientation of the stripes running through the stack.

3 Continue reducing the cane in this way until it is 4in (10cm) long, then cut the cane in half and trim off the distorted ends (see

pendant on page 80). Set one half aside (use it to make stripe patterns such as tile 25 on page 98) and continue working with the other half.

4 Compact the half cane all over to make it square. Place it on your work surface with the cut edge uppermost. Cut diagonally across the stripes of the cane. Do not separate the pieces.

It does not matter precisely where you make the diagonal cut.

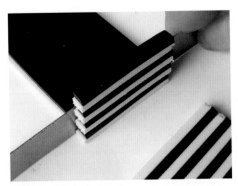

5 Roll out sheets of black and white clay, ³⁄₃₂in (2mm) thick. Cut a 1¼ x 3in (3 x 7.5cm) rectangle of each color and stack the black on top of the white. Cut an ⅛in (3mm) strip from the end of the stack, pulling the blade toward you so that the strip sticks to the blade. Use this strip on the blade to measure the next one. Continue in this way to build up a striped sheet.

6 Insert the striped sheet into the diagonal cut on the square cane. Press the three sections together and trim to make the cane square again. Roll out some yellow clay, ⅛in (3mm) thick. Make another diagonal cut through the cane and insert a piece of yellow clay. Make the cane square again.

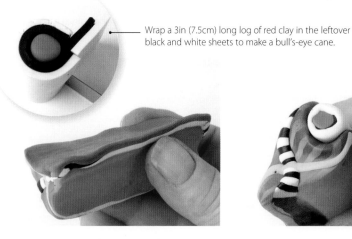

Wrap a 3in (7.5cm) long log of red clay in the leftover black and white sheets to make a bull's-eye cane.

7 Pinch one side of the square cane to form a point; this will be the bottom of the cane, so choose the side that will look best. Press the cane down onto your work surface and start reducing the cane and shaping it into a triangle (see page 81). Reduce the cane until it is about 3in (7.5cm) long.

8 With the top edge of the triangle facing up, pull out the two points to create a channel. Place a bull's-eye in the channel and wrap the extended points of the triangle around it. The points of the triangle do not have to touch at the top (it looks better when they do not).

9 Roll out a sheet of black clay, 1⁄32in (1mm) thick, and wrap it around the cane. Reduce the cane so that it is really long, pinching along the point to maintain the teardrop shape.

Building patterns

You can build up numerous patterns by altering the shape and orientation of the cane slices. If you cut a long cane into smaller sections, you can combine those sections into your chosen pattern and then cut slices from that.

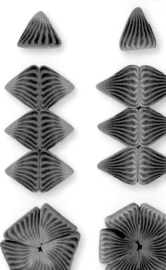

CANING & STACKING

Striated canes

Striated stacks of clay are really a type of cane, and when you cut slices off the faces of the canes you get patterns. Striated canes are particularly good for simulating natural materials such as bone, ivory and wood that have fine stripes running through them.

You will need:

- Pasta machine, roller, tissue blade and ripple blade

- Polymer clay in:
  » Translucent, white and champagne for bone/ivory
  » Brown and white for wood shingle
  » Brown, caramel, champagne, white and translucent for knotted wood

- For pearlescent ink shell:
  » Translucent and black clay
  » Pearlescent acrylic ink in purple, light blue, dark blue, turquoise, lime green and salmon pink
  » Paintbrush

Wooden bead pendant
Marie Segal
Elongated triangles of wood shingle cane are applied to a ball of scrap clay. The first layer of slices meet at the bottom; the next layer overlap the first layer and cover the top of the ball. The pendant is embellished with wire and small beads.

Maintain the color sequence throughout when stacking the sheets, with translucent on the bottom followed by white and champagne.

Bone and ivory
1 Roll out sheets of translucent, white and champagne clay, ⅛in (3mm) thick. Cut a 2in (5cm) square from each sheet and stack them together in that order. Cut in half and stack together to form a rectangular block, maintaining the color sequence.

2 Press the block together to make it flatter and then use a roller to lengthen the rectangle to about 4in (10cm). Try to keep the edges straight and square. Cut in half and stack, with cut edges together.

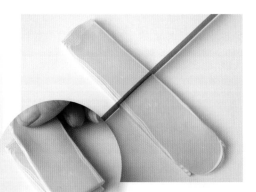

3 Use the roller to tack the two halves together and lengthen the stack to about 4in (10cm) once more. Try to keep the width to about 1½in (4cm) and the sides even. Cut in half and stack, then cut in half and stack once more. Tack together and lengthen to about 6in (15cm). Cut in half and stack, then cut in half and stack once more.

4 Even up the sides and make the stack straight and sharp. Cut in half and stack for the final time. Compact together so that the line in the middle disappears and it becomes one block. Cut slices from the end of the block.

Wood shingle

1 Roll out sheets of brown and white clay, ⅛in (3mm) thick. Cut a 1½ x 4¾in (4 x 10cm) rectangle from each sheet and stack brown on top of white. Cut the stack into thirds widthwise and stack together with colors alternating. Rolling from the center outward, flatten and lengthen the stack to about 4½in (11.5cm). Try not to widen it very much.

2 Cut in half and stack with cut edges together, maintaining the color sequence. Use the roller to tack the two halves together and lengthen the stack to about 3in (7.5cm). Cut in half and stack, then cut in half and stack once more.

Rainbow collar

Marie Segal

Although the cane used to make this necklace looks very different from the wood shingle, it is made using the same basic stacking technique. Sheets of clay in multiple colors are arranged in tonal color groups and stacked on top of each other. The rectangular stack is compressed on the diagonal by pressing on two opposite corners. The stack is then cut in half and the two halves folded down against each other to create a mirror image, and then reshaped into a rectangle. The rectangle is then lengthened, halved and stacked several times to create diagonal zigzags of color. The finished cane is shaped into a spear shape and thick slices are pierced and strung together with small beads.

3 Cut the stack in half lengthwise this time to form two roughly square halves. Rotate one half so that the newly cut edges align and then stack together.

4 Trim off any excess clay to create a neat stack, then compact the stack together to form a block that is roughly square.

5 With one of the cut ends with the striations uppermost, hold your thumb and forefinger together to form a V shape and press down on the top edges of the block, pinching them together to reshape the block into a triangle and begin lengthening it. Continue pinching and reducing the cane until the triangle measures about ¾in (2cm) and the cane is 3in (7.5cm) long or more.

The triangular slices resemble wooden roof shingles but can also be used to simulate dragon and animal scales and organic pod formations.

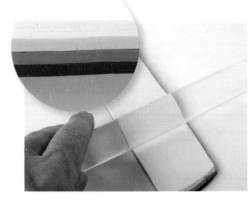

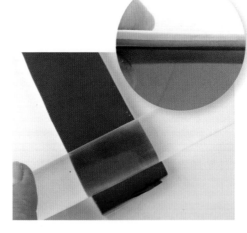

Knotted wood

1 Roll out sheets of brown, caramel, champagne and translucent clay, ⅛in (3mm) thick. Roll out a sheet of white clay, ¹⁄₃₂in (1mm) thick. Cut 2 x 6in (5 x 15cm) strips of each color and stack them in this order: brown, caramel, champagne, white and translucent. Use a roller to tack the strips together.

2 Peel the strip from your work surface, turn it over and roll on the other side. If you loosen the strip from the work surface and roll it lengthwise, it will lengthen more than widen; this is what you want to happen. Roll the strip in this way until the thickness is reduced by half.

3 Roll the strip lengthwise through a pasta machine on the thickest setting. Cut the strip in half. An easy way to find the middle is to lift up both ends of the strip so that the middle touches the work surface.

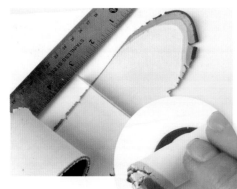

4 Cut a 3in (7.5cm) section from one end of the strip. Measure from the very end of the strip; it does not matter if the end is not straight. Starting at the cut edge, roll up into a spiral cane. White is on the outside here, but the other way works just as well. Reduce the cane to about ⅜in (1cm) thick and 10in (25cm) long.

5 Cut the spiral cane in half. Reduce one half to about ³⁄₁₆in (4.5mm) thick and 8in (20cm) long. Leave the other half as it is. Cut a 1in (2.5cm) section off the end of the long strip. Place a 1in (2.5cm) piece of each spiral cane on the end of the strip and place the cut section on top to sandwich the spirals inside.

6 Press the clay down between the spiral canes. Keep adding spiral canes randomly between sections of the long strip, adding as many "knots" and layers as you wish. Compact the block with your fingers so that everything sticks together.

Create different wood grains by varying the number of knots that you add.

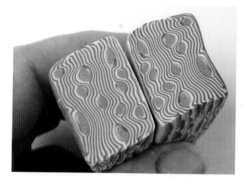

7 Compress the block by squeezing the sides. You will be compressing and lengthening the block in the same direction as the spiral canes. Continue in this way, keeping the edges straight and corners sharp. When the block is about 5in (12.5cm) long, cut in half and stack with cut edges together. Compress and lengthen again to about 4in (10cm).

8 Cut in half and stack together. Compact the two halves, but do not lengthen this time. Cut slices from the end of the block, placing them side by side and using a roller to tack them together to form larger sheets if required.

9 Wad up any excess clay and trimmings to form a ¾in (2cm) ball. Do not roll tightly so that the clay retains as many of the striations as possible. Use a skewer to pierce a hole through the bead, twisting it into the bead from one side and then the other. Stand the bead on the hole for baking. For an aged effect, apply a wash of brown acrylic.

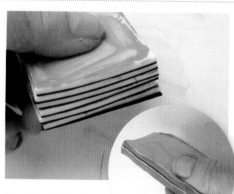

Pearlescent ink shell

1 Roll out some translucent clay, ⅛in (3mm) thick, and cut a 1½ x 9in (4 x 23cm) strip. Use a tissue blade to mark it into six equal sections, then paint each section with a different-colored ink. Use the paintbrush to dig out the thick pearly ink from the bottom of the bottle (don't shake the bottle); this is the stuff you paint with.

2 Let the ink dry (it can take a few hours). Roll out some black clay, ¹⁄₆₄in (0.5mm) thick, and lay the painted strip on top. Trim off the excess black clay, then divide into individual colored sections and stack them together, color uppermost. Flatten the stack to about ¼in (6mm) thick, then cut in half and stack together.

3 Flatten to about ¼in (6mm) thick, then cut in half and stack. Flatten to about ⅜in (1cm). Cut in half and stack, then cut in half and stack once more. Press everything together. Stand the block with cut edges uppermost and slice with a ripple blade. Roll the slices flat.

CANING & STACKING

Mokumé gané

Mokumé gané is a Japanese metalworking technique that involves folding and flattening layers of colored metals to form water-like or wood-grain patterns. In polymer clay, you can simulate this effect by stacking sheets of clay together and then distorting the stack using a variety of methods. Cutting through the stack reveals exciting patterns, and each slice of the clay will be slightly different.

You will need:

- Pasta machine, roller and tissue blade (it needs to be brand new or very sharp)
- Polymer clay in at least two colors; try adding a layer of metallic clay to the stack or translucent clay covered with metal leaf for extra richness
- Tall, round, smooth glass
- Selection of tools for distorting the stack, such as a texture sheet, small cutters, ripple blade, texture paddle, rubber sheet stamp and knitting needle
- Extruder with half-domed die

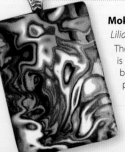

Mokumé gané pendant
Lilian Nichols
The simple rectangular shape is perfect for displaying the beautiful colors, dramatic patterns and individuality of mokumé gané.

Maintain the alternating color sequence when building the stack.

Texture sheet distortions

1 This two-color stack is made from 2in (5cm) squares of black and white clay, both ⅛in (3mm) thick. Stack one on top of the other and then roll through a pasta machine on the thickest setting. The layered sheet will now be rectangular. Cut in half widthwise and stack one on top of the other, cut edges together and colors alternating.

2 Roll the stack through the machine again, placing the cut edges into the rollers first. Halve and stack as before to give you eight layers. Spray a mist of water over a texture sheet. Place the stack of clay onto the texture sheet and then roll both through the machine together.

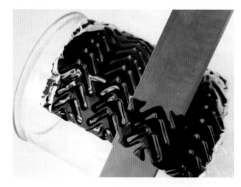

3 Peel the clay off the texture sheet and place it onto a smooth glass. Cup your palm over the clay to attach it to the glass. Use a sharp tissue blade to cut very thin slivers off the clay. Do not worry about any holes in the slivers.

4 When you turn the slivers over, you will see the mokumé gané pattern. Apply the slivers to a background sheet of clay; the background color will show through the holes in the slivers. Use a roller to flatten the slivers on the sheet. The clay that is left on the glass will also have a mokumé pattern. Roll this flat and, if it is very thin, apply it to a background sheet of clay as well.

If you accidentally cut all the way through the stack, place it onto another sheet of clay to hold everything together.

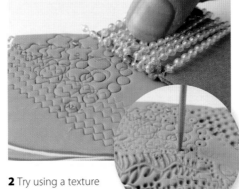

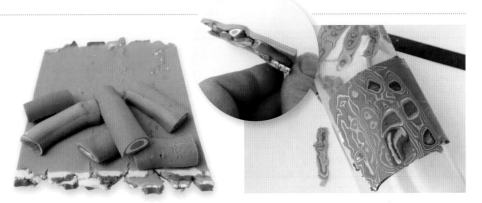

Using multiple texturing tools

1 Make an eight-layer stack of clay as before, but start with four colors in the initial stack (here, white, blue, turquoise and green). Lay the flattened stack onto your work surface and use various tools to distort it. Press small cutters in different shapes into the clay, followed by a ripple blade.

2 Try using a texture paddle (see page 55); this one is made with a string of fused plastic pearls. Texture paddles work well because they impress deeply but do not cut through. Continue distorting the stack. Here, a rubber sheet stamp and then a knitting needle are used.

3 Press the stack onto a glass and use a tissue blade to slice off thin slivers as before. Apply the slivers to a background sheet of clay and roll flat.

Adding extrusions

1 Make an eight-layer stack as described above. Roll out ⅛in (3mm) thick sheets of clay in various colors (here, blue, green, lavender, white and gray). Using the barrel of an extruder, cut out disks of each color and insert them into the barrel. Screw a half-domed die onto the end of the barrel.

2 Extrude half-moon shaped logs of clay and cut them into small pieces. Lay them randomly over one half of the layered stack.

3 Cut off the empty half of the stack and place it on top of the logs, sandwiching them inside. Press the stack around the logs. Place the stack onto a glass and cut off slices as before. The extrusions will cause distortions inside the stack and the slices will reveal sections of the extrusions.

Slivers of mokumé gané are a great way to decorate beads (see page 18).

CANING & STACKING

Tile samples

Layering different colors of clay into logs and stacks that contain patterns running through them provides a rich source of decoration for polymer clay artists. Slices of the canes can be applied as veneers to create all-over patterns or arranged as appliqué to build up three-dimensional designs. Distorting a block of layered clay, such as in mokumé gané, or using distorted ripple blades to cut through the clay is another way to create intricate decorations.

Cane flower
Marie Segal
This flower is formed from simple scrap clay shapes covered with cane slices (the cane on page 86 but in a different colorway). Even the curving leaves and outer petals are cane slices.

SPIRAL SLICES

1 Round slices
Rainbow spiral cane (see page 80) plus translucent silver clay
How-to: Apply thin slices of the cane to a sheet of translucent silver, arranging them in rows and overlapping the edge of the sheet if necessary. Use a roller to flatten the slices onto the sheet, then trim the edges. Bake and quench.

2 Diagonal slices
Rainbow spiral cane (see page 80) plus translucent gold clay
How-to: Make this in the same way as tile 1, but cut diagonal slices from the cane and apply them in offset overlapping rows.

3 Teardrop slices
Rainbow spiral cane (see page 80) plus translucent silver clay
How-to: Pinch along one side of the cane to form a teardrop shape. Apply thin slices of the cane, point downward, in offset overlapping rows to a sheet of translucent gold clay. Continue as for tile 1.

RIPPLE CUTS

4 Rainbow ripple

Rainbow spiral cane (see page 80) plus translucent gold clay
How-to: Referring to steps 6–8 on page 81, shape and stack the cane, then stand the cane on edge and use a ripple blade to cut slices. Apply slices side by side to a sheet of translucent gold clay, roll flat and then trim the edges. Bake and quench.

5 White ripple

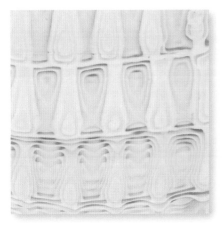

White, translucent and turquoise clay
How-to: This is made in the same way as tile 4, but using translucent in place of the rainbow blend when making the spiral cane. The ripple-cut slices are applied to a sheet of turquoise clay.

6 Metallic ripple

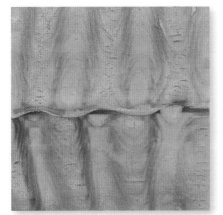

Silver, translucent, gold and champagne clay
How-to: This is made in the same way as tile 4, but the spiral cane is composed of a thin strip of silver, then a thicker strip of translucent followed by a thin top layer of gold. The ripple-cut slices are applied to a sheet of champagne clay.

FAUX SHELL

7 Basketweave shell

Faux shell cane (see page 82) plus champagne clay
How-to: Shape and stack the cane to form a basketweave pattern as described. Stand the cane on edge and use a ripple blade to cut slices. Apply to a sheet of champagne clay, roll flat, then trim the edges. Bake and quench.

8 Dark pearlized shell

Pearlescent ink shell cane (see page 91) plus champagne clay
How-to: Paint some white clay with pearlescent inks and make a striated cane stack as described. Stand on edge and use a ripple blade to cut slices. Apply to a sheet of champagne clay, then roll, trim, bake and quench.

9 Light pearlized shell

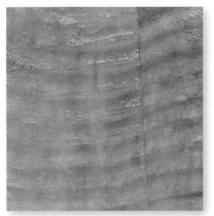

Pearlescent ink shell cane minus black clay (see page 91) plus translucent silver clay
How-to: Make this in the same way as tile 8, but omit the layer of black clay from the stack.

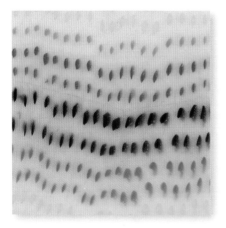

DOT PATTERNS

10 Confetti dots
Confetti dots cane (see page 83) plus white clay
How-to: Cut slices of the cane and lay side by side, maintaining the dot pattern. Use a roller to tack the slices together, then apply to a sheet of white clay. Roll again, trim the edges, bake and quench.

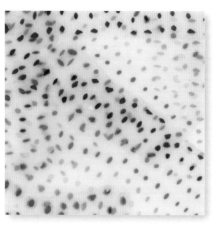

13 Random dots
Confetti dots cane (see page 83) plus white clay
How-to: Cut ultra thin slivers of the cane and use the tissue blade to transfer them onto a sheet of white clay. They do not have to be complete slices, just as thin as possible. Overlay them randomly, then roll, trim, bake and quench.

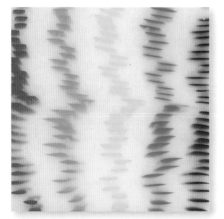

11 Machine-rolled dots
Confetti dots cane adapted as described below plus white clay
How-to: Make the cane as described on page 83, but instead of compressing and lengthening the stack by hand, pass it through a pasta machine on the thickest setting. Apply slices as for tile 10.

14 Dots on foil
Transfer foil; confetti dots cane (see page 83) plus 1:1 mixture of black and silver clay
How-to: Apply the foil to a sheet of the black/silver mixture (see page 34). Apply thin slivers of cane to the foil-covered clay in the same way as tile 13. After baking and quenching, the foil will show through the translucent clay of the cane.

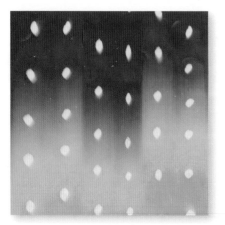

12 Reverse dots
Confetti dots cane adapted as described below plus white clay
How-to: Make the cane as described on page 83, but reverse the pattern by placing logs of white clay inside a blended sheet of translucent rainbow colors. Apply slices as for tile 10.

BULL'S-EYE PATTERNS

15 Window cane
Window cane (see page 85) plus champagne clay
How-to: Apply thin slices of cane to a sheet of champagne clay, butting them together to maintain the grid of windows and overlapping the edge of the sheet if necessary. Roll, trim, bake and quench.

16 Two-color windows

Window cane adapted as described below plus brown clay

How-to: Make the cane as described on page 85, but using two bull's-eye canes, one with a translucent red log at the center and the other with translucent blue. Wrap each log with layers of white and very pale translucent gold. Alternate the two bull's-eyes when stacking the cane.

19 Spirals and windows

Rainbow spiral cane (see page 80) and window cane (as tile 16) plus white clay

How-to: Apply slices of both canes to a sheet of white clay, overlapping them randomly. Roll flat, then trim the edges, bake and quench. The bottom layer of cane slices will show through the translucent colors of the slices that overlap them.

17 African trade tile

White, blue, black, red, yellow, green and gold clay (or any combination of strong colors)

How-to: Apply alternating rows of round and triangular bull's-eye cane slices framed by twisted and plain logs of clay at top and bottom (see page 84). Flatten with a roller, then bake.

20 Spirals and dots

Faux shell spiral cane (see page 82) and confetti dots cane (see page 83) plus translucent silver clay

How-to: Apply thin slivers of faux shell spiral cane and confetti dot cane to a sheet of translucent silver clay in overlapping layers. Roll flat, then bake and quench to enhance translucency.

CANE COLLAGE

18 Spiral collage

Faux shell spiral cane (see page 82) plus white clay

How-to: Apply thin slices of a pearlized spiral cane onto a sheet of white clay. Combine complete slices with thin slivers in overlapping layers. Roll flat, then bake and quench. The layered cane slices will show through each other.

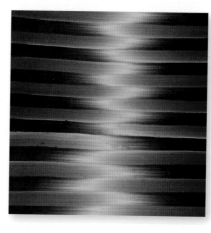

STRIPES

21 Zigzag stripes

Zigzag stripes cane (see page 85) plus brown clay

How-to: Apply slices of the cane to a sheet of brown clay, roll to tack the pieces together, then trim the edges and bake. The white at the center of the cane looks like an ombré stripe pattern on ikat fabric.

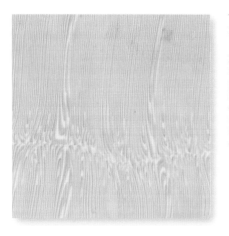

STRIATIONS

22 Bone and ivory
Bone and ivory cane (see page 88) plus white clay
How-to: Apply slices of the cane to a sheet of white clay. Roll, trim, bake and quench. If you wish, use slightly lighter or whiter colors for ivory.

23 Knotted wood
Knotted wood cane (see page 90) plus leftover clay
How-to: Apply slices of the cane to a sheet made from the leftover clay. You can change the colors to simulate different woods. Reduce the number of knots to create different wood grains, or leave them out altogether to get planking or floorboard effects. Increase the number of knots for a faux cholla cactus skeleton.

CANE APPLIQUÉ

24 Wood shingles
Wood shingle cane (see page 89) plus leftover clay
How-to: Apply triangular cane slices to a sheet made from the leftover clay. Start with a row at the bottom of the sheet, letting the points overhang. Add more rows above, offsetting and overlapping the shingles. Trim the edges and then bake.

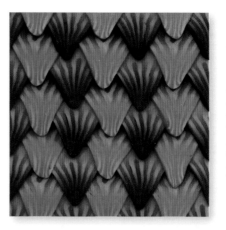

25 Striped shingles
Leftover striped cane (see page 86, step 3) plus yellow clay
How-to: Compress and lengthen the cane, then cut in half. Take one half and pinch the predominantly red side to form a triangle shape. Repeat with the second half but pinch the predominantly blue side. Apply cane slices to a sheet of yellow clay as for tile 24, alternating and offsetting the two cane sections.

26 Cane flower
"Between the spaces" cane (see page 86) plus blue and red clay
How-to: Apply eight cane slices to a square of blue clay, pointing north, south, east, west and to each corner. Apply a circle of overlapping slices on top, with the points going into the spaces between the lower slices. Press a ball of red clay into the center, indenting it in the middle, then bake.

27 Cane border
"Between the spaces" cane (see page 86) plus blue and black clay
How-to: Apply a focal piece of six cane slices in the center of a square of blue clay. Flatten the remaining cane into a triangular shape and use it to create a straight-edged border (see building patterns, page 87). Apply an extra cane slice on top of each corner. Press small balls of black clay inside each corner, indent them and then bake.

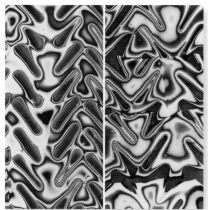

Sliced sheet (left) and cut-off slivers applied to lavender clay (right).

MOKUMÉ GANÉ

28 Texture sheet

Black and white stack (see page 92) plus lavender clay

How-to: Roll the stack through a pasta machine with a texture sheet to distort the clay. Press the distorted stack onto a glass and then cut off slivers. Remove the sliced sheet from the glass and roll flat; apply the slivers to a sheet of lavender clay and roll flat. Bake both.

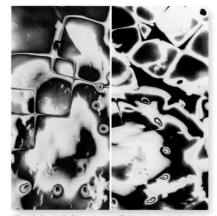

Sliced sheet (left) and cut-off slivers applied to black clay (right).

31 Cutters

Black and white stack (see page 92) plus black clay

How-to: Use several cutters in different shapes—here, square, oval and star cutters—to distort the stack, then poke the stack with a knitting needle. Continue as for tile 28.

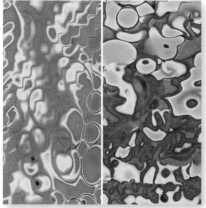

Sliced sheet (left) and cut-off slivers applied to lavender clay (right).

29 Texturing tools

Color stack (see page 93) plus lavender clay

How-to: Use a variety of texturing tools to distort the stack, pressing them randomly all over. Several cutters, a ripple blade, texture paddle, texture sheet and knitting needle are used here. Continue as for tile 28.

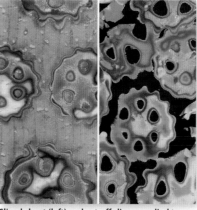

Sliced sheet (left) and cut-off slivers applied to black clay (right).

32 Canes and gears

Color stack adapted as described below plus black clay

How-to: Make the stack as described on page 93 but using violet, turquoise, blue and translucent with a sheet of gold leaf applied to it. Add round slices from a spiral cane made from an orange to white blend. Continue as for tile 28. The texture sheet used here featured gear wheels.

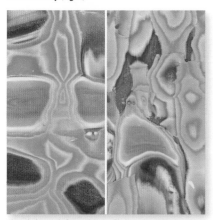

Sliced sheet (left) and cut-off slivers applied to lavender clay (right).

30 Extrusions

Color stack and half-moon extrusions (see page 93) plus lavender clay

How-to: Lay the extrusions randomly over half of the stack, then place the empty half of the stack on top to sandwich the extrusions in between. Flatten, apply to a glass and then cut off slivers and continue as for tile 28.

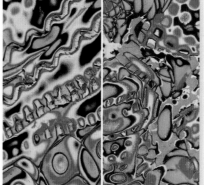

Sliced sheet (left) and cut-off slivers applied to gold clay (right).

33 Cake-decorating tools

Color stack adapted as described below plus gold clay

How-to: Make the stack as described on page 93 but using red, pearl, black and gold. Also add a thinner sheet of white clay. Distort the stack using various tools; here, heart-shaped and round cutters, a cake-decorating rolling tool with dashed and zigzag wheels, and a knitting needle and large ball stylus. Continue as for tile 28.

CANING & STACKING

Polymer clay artists at work

The decorative techniques displayed here—cane slices reshaped and assembled into patterns, striated faux effects such as wood and ivory, blended stripe patterns and mokumé gané effects cut from distorted stacks of layered clay—are used by polymer clay artists to produce beautiful veneers for embellishing clay beads and other forms. Simple canes—spirals, dots, bull's-eyes and striated blocks—can be combined in a multitude of ways to make complex-looking decorations.

» See pages 94–99 for tile samples

◄ Crust pendant
Izabela Nowak

Techniques used: This 3½ x 3½in (9 x 9cm) organic, freeform pendant was inspired by nature and the artist's desire to play with color and structure to create something that can conform to whatever shape each individual likes. The bone and ivory cane on page 88 can be adapted to create colorful striations by using many more colors in the stack. When flattening and reducing the stack, work slowly and carefully to keep the lines of color as straight as possible. Slices of the cane can then be wrapped around a pre-formed shape in lightweight polymer clay.
See STRIATIONS tile 22

► Faux abalone spirit box
Mags Bonham

Techniques used: Sheets of faux abalone are formed into a pillow-shaped box set on a pedestal with a spire of beads on top. The faux abalone is created using the mokumé gané technique, combining translucent, metallic and acrylic-painted sheets of clay. Tinting silver clay with a bit of blue, green, turquoise and violet would give you a wonderful stack for making faux abalone. You could also add a very thin sheet of white clay painted with black acrylic, a sheet of translucent covered with silver leaf or translucent tinted with alcohol ink.
See MOKUMÉ GANÉ tiles 28–33

▲ Rainbow ripple bangle
Marie Segal

Techniques used: A confetti dots cane with dots of white clay embedded into a blended sheet of translucent rainbow colors is used to make this 4in (10cm) diameter bangle. Slices of the cane are applied around a log of plain clay, with all of the joins aligned along one side of the log. The decorated log is then glued into the channel of a brass bangle blank, with the joins hidden on the inside. The ends of the log are pressed together, and then a fluted edge is created by pinching along the log with a finger and thumb. A thin log of white clay is applied around the fluted edge before baking and quenching.
See DOT PATTERNS tile 12

◀ **Petal ornament**
Nancy Nearing
Techniques used: This organic pod formation is created by applying slices of a leaf cane over a heart-shaped glass Christmas ornament in a symmetrical arrangement. The leaf cane is made from a grayed-out turquoise Skinner blend shaded to dark teal, with copper and black veins and edging. Matte Swarovski hot-fix pearls are embedded into the tip of each cane slice before applying it to the ornament. The hanging loop is made from brass wire. The ornament measures approximately 2½in (6.5cm) high and 2in (5cm) at the widest point.
See CANE APPLIQUÉ tiles 24–25

▲ **Sea homes necklace**
Anna Maria Gray
Techniques used: This necklace was inspired by sea life and patterns in seashells, as well as the seashell as a protective environment. The 4½ x ¾in (11.5 x 2cm) pods are made from slices of lace cane wrapped around a removable core to create a hollow pod. A metallic bead nestles within each pod. Lace canes are simply patterns of repeated bull's-eyes. To make a simple lace cane, cut a reduced bull's-eye cane into seven equal lengths and bundle six of the pieces around the seventh. Roll and compress. Whereas in a window cane the bull's-eyes are maintained in a square shape, in a lace cane the bull's-eyes become distorted into irregular shapes.
See BULL'S-EYE PATTERNS tiles 15–17

▼ **Faux ivory scarf pin**
Mags Bonham
Techniques used: Faux ivory made with opaque and translucent polymer clay is cut into the shape of a large paisley design. It is then textured with assorted tools and antiqued with acrylic paint. A stick pin is embedded between two leaf shapes cut from the faux ivory clay. This scarf pin would also look good using faux wood.
See STRIATIONS tiles 22–23

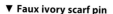

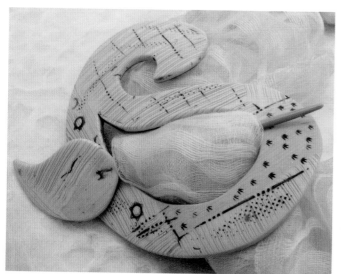

▶ **Wooden bangle**
Marie Segal
Techniques used:
A combination of three different effects are combined on this 3¾in (9.5cm) diameter bangle: slices of faux wood and zigzag stripe canes, plus Sutton slice (see page 110). Veneers of the three effects are added in sections around a log of scrap clay and rolled until smooth. PVA glue is added to the center of a bangle blank and then the log of decorative clay is applied, smoothed into shape and baked.
See STRIPES tile 21 and STRIATIONS tile 23

▼ **Starfish pendant**

Kathy Dummer

Techniques used: Simple bull's-eye canes in various sizes are combined to build up the intricate bull's-eye patterns of this 2⅛in (5.5cm) diameter starfish. Each leg of the starfish is cut from the same bull's-eye pattern, while the center is cut from another. The slightly raised green dots are liquid polymer clay tinted with mica powder applied over white clay dots in the cane pattern below, giving the illusion of texture as well as simulating the beautiful radiating pattern of ossicles on an actual starfish.

See BULL'S-EYE PATTERNS tiles 15–17

▼ **Multi-caned veneered beads**

Karen Lewis

Techniques used: Slices from many different complex canes are applied in overlapping layers and then rolled together until smooth on the surface. After baking, the beads are sanded and buffed meticulously to give them a high-gloss, glass-like finish. The plentiful and beautiful cane slices combine both opaque and translucent clays to build up a symphony of color and pattern. The beads are made in a variety of shapes and measure around 1–1½in (2.5–4cm).

See CANE COLLAGE tiles 18–20

◀ **Crown basket**

Victoria James

Techniques used: This 6in (15cm) high mixed media piece consists of a coiled basket with a polymer clay base and rim. The base and rim are slab-constructed, layered polymer clay. The middle part is a coil-constructed basket of Jeffery pine needles. The technique used here is texture sheet mokumé gané, in which thin layers of pearlescent polymer clay are rolled into a sheet. Mica powder is applied to the top of the sheet, then a texture is impressed into it. The raised areas are removed with a blade to reveal the layers beneath.

See MOKUMÉ GANÉ tiles 28–33

◀ Hexagon bangles
Carol Blackburn

Techniques used: Trianglular slices of black and white blended stripes are cut and applied to the bangle form in a hexagonal design where the stripes appear to rotate around the bangle. A strip of black clay is applied around the outside edge. The striped cane can be made in a similar way to the zigzag stripes on page 85 but without flipping the colors. Each bangle is 4½in (11.5cm) diameter from point to point.

See STRIPES tile 21

◀ Summer eleven necklace
Martina Medenica

Techniques used: Each triangular bead features a collage of different cane slices, including geometric and flower canes in translucent and opaque colors. The surface of the beads is coated with UV resin for a glossy finish. One way of building up multilayered designs is to apply cane slices to a master sheet of translucent clay, without overlapping the slices, and then roll it flat. You can make several master sheets, and then cut out and layer pieces on top of each other on a background piece of clay. Each bead measures 1½in (4cm) and the necklace is 18in (45cm) long.

See CANE COLLAGE tiles 18–20

▲ Atlantis segment cuff
Martina Medenica

Techniques used: This bracelet is a wonderful example of the water patterns that can be created with mokumé gané. Layered slices of mokumé gané are applied to buff-colored clay to form the 2½ x 1¼in (6.5 x 3cm) segments of the bracelet. The name of the piece is in perfect harmony with the rippling patterns and marine colors. You could try a set of fire-like colors for a totally different look.

See MOKUMÉ GANÉ tiles 28–33

Between the spaces necklace
Marie Segal

Techniques used: Slices from the "Between the spaces" complex cane (see page 86; this one is made in a different colorway) are carefully pressed onto a sheet of glass to give them a very smooth, glass-like surface when they are baked. A black clay tube bead is attached to the back of each cane slice with liquid clay before baking. The baked beads are strung together on a rubber cord to make a simple but striking 30in (76cm) long necklace.

See CANE APPLIQUÉ tiles 26–27

PATTERNS & MOTIFS

Mica shift

Some metallic polymer clays contain mica particles. When the clay is rolled so that the particles are aligned, the mica reflects light to give the clay a shiny metallic look. In contrast, when you cut through the clay, the side edges look dull. Various methods—such as impressing, cutting and twisting—are used to combine the dull and the shiny to produce chatoyant effects that look three-dimensional but are actually flat patterns within the clay. The effect looks more pronounced after baking and quenching.

You will need:

- Pasta machine, roller, tissue blade and ripple blade
- Polymer clay containing mica; try using a 1:1 mix of mica and translucent clay to enhance the chatoyant effect
- Texture sheet or rubber stamp

Square bead necklace
Carol Blackburn
The mica clay beads are smooth and flat, but retain ghost images of impressed textures.

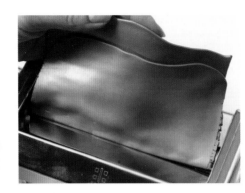

Aligning the mica particles
The first stage for all mica shift effects is to align the mica particles. To do this, roll the clay through a pasta machine on the thickest setting (or roll by hand if you prefer), then fold in half and roll again. Repeat this several times, always folding and rolling the clay in the same direction, until the surface has a reflective satin sheen.

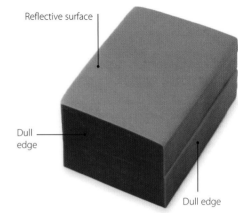

Reflective surface

Dull edge

Dull edge

Stacked sheets
When sheets of mica clay are cut and stacked into a block, you can see the effect of the aligned mica particles. The top and bottom surfaces have a satin sheen, while the side edges are dull and appear to be darker.

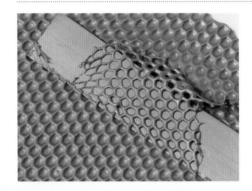

Ghost impressions
Use a texture sheet or rubber stamp (misted with water or a release agent to prevent sticking) to impress a pattern or image into a thick sheet of mica clay. Holding a tissue blade horizontally, slice off the textured surface of the clay. Roll the sheet flat to create a smooth surface that retains a ghost image of the impressed pattern.

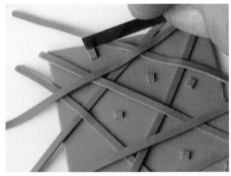

Sticks and stones
Use a tissue blade to cut thin slices from the edge of a sheet of mica clay and apply them to another sheet, crisscrossing the strips and placing them dull side down. Cut one of the slices into little squares and use the blade to apply those between the strips. Use a roller to press the pieces into the sheet, turning the sheet 90 degrees every time you roll it.

Shiny V shape

Dull V shape

Knit stitches

1 Cut two strips of mica clay of equal width and thickness. Holding down one end of the first strip, use a forefinger to roll the other end toward you to twist the strip. Repeat with the second strip, rolling in the opposite direction. Place the two strips side by side so that the shiny and dull sections form V shapes.

2 Lightly tack pairs of strips together at each end, then place them onto a sheet of mica clay. Press the strips into the sheet using a roller, starting gently and applying more pressure each time you roll. Roll lengthwise along the strips to retain the V-shaped knit stitch pattern. Roll through a pasta machine to smooth completely, then trim the edges.

Twisted spirals

Twist single strips of mica clay as for knit stitches, but twisting them all in the same direction. Wind them into spirals and press onto a sheet of mica clay. Offset each row and use half spirals at row ends. Finish as for knit stitches, but turn the sheet 90 degrees each time you roll it. Alternatively, leave the spirals raised on the surface for a filigree effect.

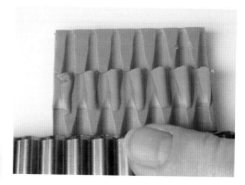

Ripple cut

Fold a sheet of mica clay in half to double the thickness to about ¼in (6mm). Holding a ripple blade horizontally, slice across the top surface of the clay. Keep the sliced strips on the blade, then flip the blade over to lay the slices onto another sheet of mica clay. Roll both sheets of clay until smooth, rolling lengthwise only.

Cut and fold

1 This is a variation on the plain ripple cut. Holding the blade at a very slight angle, cut into the top layer of the clay so that you have little tabs of clay reaching about three-quarters of the way up the blade. Fold the blade over and press the little tabs down onto the clay sheet.

2 Start the next cut directly below the pressed-down tabs of clay from the first cut. Place the recesses of the blade into the spaces between the folded tabs. Fold over and press down the next row of tabs as before. Continue over the whole piece, then roll flat as for the plain ripple cut.

PATTERNS & MOTIFS

Extrusions

An extruder can be one of the polymer clay artist's most valuable tools. Here, extruded strings of clay are used to create inlaid patterns of graphic dots and stripes, and then a raised spiral design. Although the latter is time-consuming, after baking you can make a mold of the design and use it to emboss other pieces with the same pattern. Softer clay is easier to extrude, so condition it well.

You will need:

- Polymer clay in black, white and gold
- Roller
- Extruder and small screen die
- Two tissue blades and ceramic tile
- Ball stylus and needle tool

Extruder and dies
The numerous dies available allow you to extrude many different shapes of clay. The bigger the die opening, the more clay that is needed, but don't fill the extruder because any clay left in the barrel will stiffen up and be harder to extrude later.

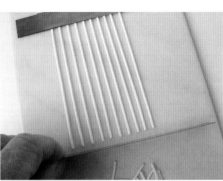

Dots and stripes
1 Insert a plug of white clay into the barrel of the extruder. Insert a small screen die into the end cap and screw it onto the barrel. Extrude strings of clay through the die, letting them fall loosely onto the work surface. Use a tissue blade to slice off the strings from the extruder.

2 Line up strings of extruded clay on a ceramic tile. Use a fingertip to press the top of each string to the tile and then pull on the other end to straighten it out. Lightly press a tissue blade across the top of the strings to hold them in place (take care not to cut through them). Use a second blade to trim the other ends level.

3 Use the second blade to cut a row of dots from the ends of the strings. Drag the blade forward slowly so that the dots stick to the blade in a row. Pick up the blade and place the dots onto a sheet of black clay. Lay the blade flat so that the dots stick to the clay below. Continue adding rows of dots in this way. Lightly roll with a roller, then turn the sheet 90 degrees and roll again. Trim any dots that overlap the edges.

4 Cut another sheet of black clay and place it over the remaining strings, either vertically or diagonally. Press the sheet down gently, then lightly roll in the direction of the strings. Slide the blade under the strings to release them from the ceramic tile, then trim the edges.

Extrude strings of gold clay in the same way as for the dots and stripes opposite, but using a slightly smaller screen die.

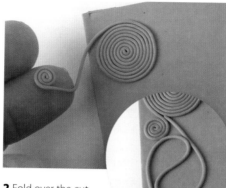

Embossed spirals

1 Pull out one string of extruded gold clay, fold the end over by ⅛in (3mm) or less and wind it up into a small spiral. Place the spiral onto a sheet of gold clay. Press it gently into place and then continue winding the spiral until it is the size you want. Trim the end of the string about 2½in (6.5cm) from the spiral.

2 Fold over the cut end by ⅛in (3mm) or less and then wind it into a spiral right up to the first spiral made. Place the small spiral onto the clay sheet. Cut the end of another string at an angle and place the point between the spirals. Arrange the string into a decorative shape and trim the end.

3 Take another string, cut off ⅛in (3mm) pieces and roll them into balls. Sometimes the cut pieces will stick to the blade and you can use the last one to measure the next one. You can often cut quite a few before they fall off, and you can cut pieces from more than one string at a time to speed things up. Place the balls onto the clay wherever you like and indent with a ball tool.

4 Lay some straight strings across the clay, pressing them down gently. Apply two or three and then trim. If the strings stick to the blade when trimming, you can lift the strings by the trimmed ends and lay them across the clay—this all saves time.

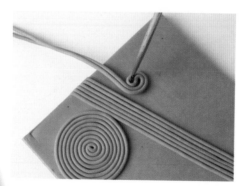

5 Another way to make a spiral is to fold a string in half. Use a needle tool to hold the folded center and start to coil the string around it. You can then place it onto the clay and continue coiling the spiral. Continue building up the embossed design in this way until you are happy with the result.

Basket of flowers brooch
Anna Maria Gray
Loading the extruder barrel with plugs of clay in different metallic colors will give you variegated strands like those adorning this filigree brooch. Metallic clay is also used for the sculpted flowers and the design is highlighted by wire and metallic beads.

PATTERNS & MOTIFS

Carving

Designs can be carved into raw or baked polymer clay. For extra color, carve through layers of different-colored clays that have been stacked and rolled together. Alternatively, backfill the carved design with another color. A very simple technique is to use cutters to create a faux carved effect. If you use the colors shown here and antique the design with a wash of acrylic paint, the finished piece will look like bone or ivory carving.

You will need:

- Pasta machine or roller and tissue blade

- For cutter carving:
  » Champagne, white and translucent clay
  » Selection of small cutters and knitting needle
  » Brown acrylic paint and stencil brush

- For carving and backfilling:
  » Black and gold clay
  » Carving tools and teaspoon
  » Sandpaper (400 and 800 grit)
  » Dorland's wax medium (or similar) and soft cloth (optional)

To simulate the color of bone or ivory, mix equal parts champagne and white clay, then mix this with an equal quantity of translucent clay. Alternatively, use a sheet of faux bone/ivory cane (see page 88).

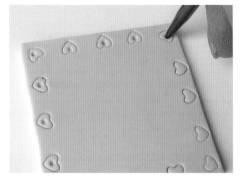

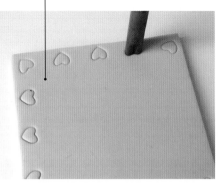

Cutter carving

1 Roll out a sheet of clay, ⅛in (3mm) thick, and cut out a small tile to decorate. Use a small heart cutter (or other shape of your choosing) to mark a border design. Start with a heart in each corner and then in the middle of each side to help you achieve even spacing.

2 Continue all around the tile with the cutter, impressing the design but taking care not to cut all the way through the clay. Use a knitting needle to indent a dot in the center of each heart. Again, impress the dots to make a mark but do not press all the way through.

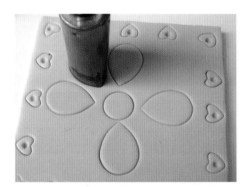

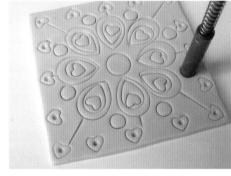

3 Use round and teardrop cutters to mark a pattern in the middle of the tile (here, a stylized flower). Mark the center circle first, then add the north, south, east and west teardrops and then the remaining teardrops. Working in this way will help you to keep the design fairly symmetrical, but it does not have to be perfect because the idea is to imitate hand carving.

4 Continue impressing the tile with cutters to build up a pleasing design. Use a knife blade to mark straight lines if you wish. Bake the tile and allow to cool. Antique the tile with a wash of brown acrylic, wiping off the excess to leave color in the carved markings only (see page 32). The finished tile will look like an old piece of hand-carved bone or ivory.

Try other colors as well as bone/ivory (see tile 21, page 40).

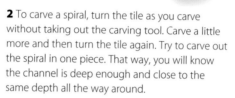

Carving and backfilling

1 Use carving or linoleum cutting tools to carve a design into baked clay. Carve the design deeply and try to keep the edges of the carved lines neat and clean. Always carve away from yourself and never hold the piece you are carving with your hand in front of the cutting blade. Work slowly and carefully.

2 To carve a spiral, turn the tile as you carve without taking out the carving tool. Carve a little more and then turn the tile again. Try to carve out the spiral in one piece. That way, you will know the channel is deep enough and close to the same depth all the way around.

3 Roll out a small log of gold clay (or other contrasting color) and press it into one of the carved grooves. Use the back of a spoon to press the soft clay into the carved lines in the baked clay. Burnish it in by rubbing the spoon over the clay again and again. Continue adding logs of clay to all of the carved lines, making sure that they are well-filled.

4 Now use the edge of the spoon to scrape off the excess clay. Keep double-checking whether you need to add more clay to any of the carved lines. Once you are satisfied that they are all filled, use the spoon to scrape off as much excess clay as you can.

5 Bake the finished piece and allow to cool. Sand the surface with 400-grit sandpaper to make sure that there is no remaining gold clay outside of the carved lines. Sand again with 800-grit paper for a smooth finish. If you wish, rub some wax medium onto the tile and then buff with a soft cloth to give the tile a soft sheen.

Carving through colored layers

When several sheets of different-colored clays are stacked and rolled together, you can carve through the layers to reveal the different colors in the carved lines of the design. You can do this before or after baking. Save any carving scraps to use as inclusions (see page 27).

PATTERNS & MOTIFS

Appliqué motifs

Sutton slice involves filling a rubber stamp with clay, slicing off the excess and then pressing the stamp onto a clay sheet to transfer the clay pattern. The clay can be left on the surface for a textured pattern or rolled flat. Logs of colored clay can be used to create raised motifs, with the logs simulating the colored enclosures found in cloisonné. After baking, you could also fill the spaces with grout to form a mosaic design.

You will need:

- Pasta machine (optional), roller and tissue blade
- For Sutton slice:
  » Polymer clay in contrasting colors such as brown and white
  » Deeply etched rubber stamp (gray rubber shows up the clay well)
  » Kitchen spoon
- For clay cloisonné:
  » Polymer clay in ocher, turquoise, violet and yellow
  » Gold mica powder

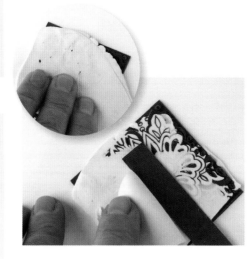

Sutton slice

1 Roll out a sheet of white clay, ⅛in (3mm) thick. Lay the clay over a rubber stamp and press it in well. Holding a tissue blade horizontally against the stamp, start slicing off the clay from the surface, a little at a time. Some clay should remain in the indentations of the stamp. If you pull some out, press the clay back in and slice it off again.

2 Do not hold the blade at too much of an angle when you slice off the clay. Glide the blade over the surface of the stamp a little at a time. The blade will be almost flat when you do this. It is not as easy to cut the stamp as you might think. Look for areas where the clay is thicker, such as over the center of this flower, and keep slicing off the clay until you can see the pattern of the stamp clearly.

3 Lay a sheet of brown clay on your work surface and place the rubber stamp face down on top. Forcefully roll over the stamp once. Don't roll back and forth.

Sutton disk pendant
Marie Segal

A white clay pattern is applied to a sheet of translucent using the Sutton slice technique. This is rolled flat and applied to a sheet of blended clay in rainbow colors, then cut to shape, baked and quenched.

4 Peel back the stamp slowly to release the clay from the stamp. Go slowly so that you can replace the stamp over the clay if you can see that some of the white clay has remained stuck in the stamp. It is much harder to line everything up if you remove the stamp completely. Either leave the pattern raised or roll it into the background sheet, then bake.

Cloisonné bead necklace
Marie Segal

The clay cloisonné technique is used to embellish the round beads and main pendant on this necklace. The symmetrical color placement of the round beads lead the eye to the focal pendant. The plain tube beads are made using an extruder with a core adapter and round die for extruding hollow shapes.

Clay cloisonné

1 Roll out some ocher clay, ⅛in (3mm) thick, and cut out a small tile to decorate. Use the end of a tissue blade to take some mica powder out of the jar and put it onto a piece of paper. Spread the powder out in a line about 5in (12.5cm) long, making sure there are no clumps.

2 Roll a log of turquoise clay, ¼in (6mm) thick and 5in (12.5cm) long. Roll the log in the powder until it is completely and thickly covered. Rub the powder into the log to make sure that it is stuck in the surface of the clay, then rub off the excess.

3 Spread out more powder and coat a log of violet and yellow clay as before. Cut all three logs in half and set one half of each aside. These logs will be left round. With the remaining half logs, press down all along one side of each log to shape it into a teardrop.

4 Use the tissue blade to cut ½₃₂in (1mm) slices from both the round and teardrop logs. Place the slices onto the ocher tile to form a pattern (here, a simple flower motif). If you get too much powder on your fingers, wipe them off so that you do not transfer too much of it to the colored surfaces of the logs.

5 Fill the tile with log slices or leave the design open, as here. Turn the tile over and trim any log slices that go over the edges of the tile, then bake.

PATTERNS & MOTIFS

Liquid clay

Liquid clay can be used to create a variety of decorative effects. Sgraffito is a plaster and ceramic technique but works very well with liquid clay. A rubber texture comb can be used to manipulate liquid clay as well as to texture the surface of polymer clay. You can create feathered effects by using a needle tool to drag liquid clay of one color through another.

You will need:

- Polymer clay pieces to be decorated
- Liquid clay, oil paints in various colors, mineral oil, paper cup or mixing palette, bamboo skewer and paintbrush
- Wire stylus and sgraffito tool
- Rubber texture comb
- Needle tools, such as knitting needle, toothpick or darning needle
- Denatured alcohol and paper towel for cleaning paintbrush and tools; rinse in soapy water afterward to remove cleaning fluids

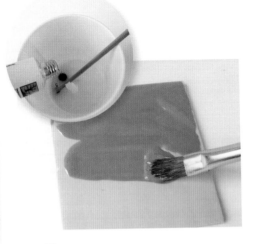

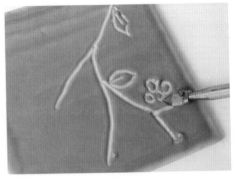

Sgraffito

1 Pour some liquid clay into a paper cup and add a small amount of oil paint to create the color you want. Stir together with a skewer, then add a couple of drops of mineral oil to reduce viscosity. Paint the colored liquid clay onto the piece you wish to decorate, then set aside in a disposable plastic container overnight.

2 Wire tools of all kinds, such as this wire stylus, can be used to draw lines through the liquid clay. Plan your design on paper beforehand, making the design simple to begin with until you get a feel for how liquid clay behaves. Try not to drag the sheet of polymer clay below, just the liquid clay. Wipe off the tool with a paper towel after making each line.

3 Work slowly and steadily, drawing a little bit of the design at a time. If you make a mistake, simply cover it with more liquid clay.

Stained-glass leaf

Sue Heaser

Thin strips of polymer clay are placed onto a sheet of glass to form the outline of the leaf design. The spaces are filled with liquid clay colored with oil paint, then a darning needle is used to create delicate feathering effects. The piece is baked on the glass.

4 Double-ended sgraffito tools are very useful. This one has two metal prongs at one end, which allows you to draw two lines at the same time and is useful for filling in the background. The other end has a spatula with a fine tip that is good for drawing fine lines. Bake as soon as you have finished the design.

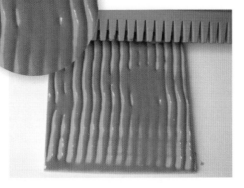

There is too much liquid clay if it flows into the combed lines, so remove the excess and try again.

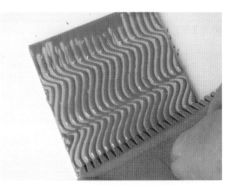

Yellow blossom pendant

Alynne Landers

Red, yellow and orange liquid clay are mixed with opaque white liquid clay and feathered to produce this flowering effect. An oval-cut piece is set in a manufactured bezel with a high-gloss UV resin finish.

Combing

1 Apply the liquid clay as for sgraffito. Drag a rubber comb across the surface in a single, gliding stroke. If you have applied too much liquid clay, it will flow back into the spaces made by the comb teeth. If that happens, simply drag the comb over the surface a few times and wipe the liquid off the comb each time to remove the excess.

2 Try making different patterns with the comb, such as squiggles, circles or large sweeping arcs from one edge to another. Many rubbers combs have several tooth widths on the same tool, so experiment with them all. Bake the finished piece as soon as you have finished the strokes.

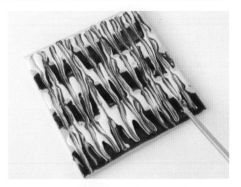

Dragging and feathering

1 Using a toothpick or paintbrush, apply horizontal stripes of liquid clay in alternating colors. Spread the liquid clay as evenly as you can. Varying the amount of liquid clay you apply and the type of needle tool you use will produce different results.

2 Try dragging a knitting needle through the liquid clay in vertical lines spaced about ¼in (6mm) apart. For finer lines, use a finer tool such as a toothpick or darning needle. A wide-toothed hair comb can be used to drag all the lines in one go. Wipe off the tool with a paper towel when you have finished each dragged line.

3 Rotate the clay sheet 180 degrees and drag vertical lines in the spaces between the first set of lines to create a feathered pattern. Bake and allow to cool completely before touching. Sometimes it is fun to leave the sheet for a little while before baking to allow the different colors of liquid clay to bleed into each other.

PATTERNS & MOTIFS

Tile samples

These tile samples show some of the many effects that can be created with simple patterning techniques. Taking advantage of mica shift effects, for example, is a fun and easy way to start making dramatic pieces, with many styles, patterns and looks being achievable with only one color of clay. Play around with the different pattern effects to build up your skills and knowledge, as well as your toolbox. Once you have tried each technique on its own, you can then start to combine them and experiment with confidence.

Ripple-effect bangle
Carol Blackburn
This ripple-cut bangle in layered mica clay combines mica shift effects, ripple blade techniques and layering, showing how a few simple techniques can be combined to create beautiful designs.

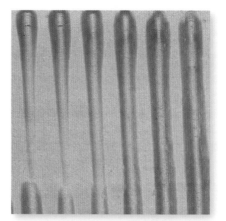

MICA SHIFT

1 Ripple cut
1 part silver mica clay mixed with 1 part translucent
How-to: Roll out a sheet of clay and fold in half. Holding a ripple blade horizontally, slice across the top of the clay, then roll flat (see page 105). Apply the cut-off slices to another sheet and roll flat to produce the same effect. You can also stand a block of stacked sheets (see page 104) on its side and cut slices with a ripple blade.

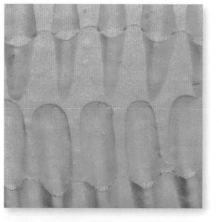

2 Cut and fold
1 part gold mica clay mixed with 1 part translucent
How-to: Roll out a sheet of clay and fold in half. Holding a ripple blade at a slight angle above horizontal, slice into the top layer of the clay, then fold over the cut tabs of clay and press onto the sheet (see page 105). Repeat across the whole sheet and then roll flat.

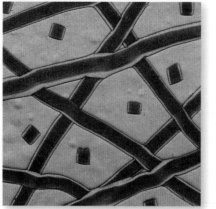

3 Sticks and stones
1 part silver mica clay mixed with 1 part translucent
How-to: Cut strips of clay and apply them in a random pattern to a sheet of clay, placing the cut edges of the strips face down. Cut a strip into small squares and apply them in the spaces, then roll flat (see page 104).

4 Knit stitches
1 part silver mica clay mixed with 1 part translucent
How-to: Twist one strip of clay in one direction and another strip in the opposite direction, then place the strips together to form the V shape of knit stitches (see page 105). Lay pairs of twisted strips onto a sheet of clay and then roll flat.

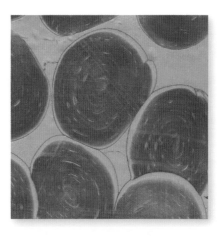

7 Sliced log
1 part gold mica clay mixed with 1 part translucent
How-to: Roll a log of clay, about ½in (13mm) diameter, and cut off thin slices. Apply the slices to a sheet of clay and then roll flat.

Lilac spirals (left) and gold spirals (right).

5 Twisted spirals
1 part silver mica mixed with 1 part translucent and 2 parts translucent lilac clay; alternative colorway: 1 part gold mica clay mixed with 1 part translucent
How-to: Twist strips of clay, all in the same direction, and then wind the strips into spirals (see page 105). Place the spirals onto a sheet of clay and then roll flat.

8 Starburst
Skinner blend of silver mica and turquoise clay (see page 20), plus 1 part silver mica clay mixed with 1 part translucent
How-to: Roll the Skinner blend very thinly, then accordion fold it back and forth to build a stack. Flatten to ¼in (6mm) thick, cut in half and place both halves together with silver on the inside. Flatten to ⅛in (3mm) thick. Apply slices to a sheet of the silver/translucent mixture in a starburst pattern, then roll flat.

6 Twisted strips
1 part silver mica mixed with 1 part translucent and 2 parts turquoise clay
How-to: Twist strips of clay in the same way as for tile 5, but leave them straight rather than winding them into spirals. Place the strips one at a time onto a sheet of clay, then roll flat.

9 Ghost impression
1 part silver mica clay mixed with 1 part translucent
How-to: Roll out a sheet of clay and fold in half. Press a stamp deeply into the clay, then shave off the high spots with a tissue blade and roll flat (see page 104).

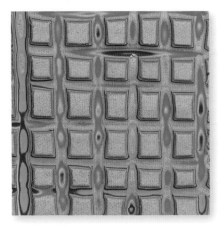

RIPPLE-CUT LAYERS

10 Multicolored grid
Flattened stack of colored clay sheets with silver on top
How-to: Holding a ripple blade horizontally, slice across the top of the clay stack to reveal the colored layers below. Turn the stack 90 degrees and slice again to form a grid pattern. You can leave the clay as it is for a three-dimensional pattern or roll it flat.

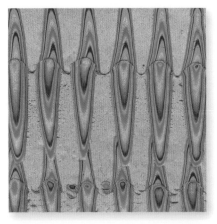

11 Multicolored ripples
Flattened stack of colored clay sheets with silver on top
How-to: Use a ripple blade and the cut-and-fold technique as described for tile 2, then roll flat.

BLOCK PATTERNS

12 Quilt block
Gold leaf; leftover patterned and plain clay scraps
How-to: Roll out a medium thick sheet of clay to use as a background. Roll out the scrap clays to the same thickness and apply gold leaf to a few of them. Cut different shapes of scrap clay and place them onto the background sheet to form a pattern. Use cutters to cut out small motifs such as flowers.

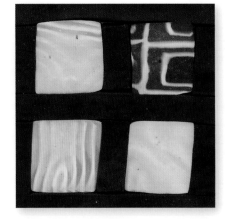

13 Translucent squares
Leftover translucent canes, color mixes or other patterned scraps, plus brown clay
How-to: Roll out a medium thick sheet of brown clay to use as a background. Roll out the translucent scraps to the same thickness and cut out squares using a cutter. Create a grid pattern of translucent squares bordered by strips of brown clay. Use a roller to attach everything together.

CARVING

14 Backfilled motifs
Dorland's wax medium (or similar); black and gold clay
How-to: Carve a design in a sheet of baked black clay, then fill the carved lines with gold clay and rebake (see page 109). Sand and then wax the finished tile to give it a sheen.

15 Sgraffito
Brown and white oil paint and liquid clay; champagne clay
How-to: Mix a small amount of brown and white oil paint into the liquid clay, then apply the mixture to a sheet of champagne clay. Use various scribing tools to draw a design through the liquid clay, then bake (see page 112).

See page 40 for alternative colorway.

16 Bone carving

Brown acrylic; mixture of 1 part champagne, 1 part white and 2 parts translucent clay
How-to: Roll out a sheet of clay and use a selection of small cutters to carve a design into the clay (see page 108). After baking, apply a wash of brown acrylic, then wipe off the excess to give the pattern the look of antique hand-carved bone.

19 Delftware

Blue, translucent and white clay
How-to: Make this in the same way as tile 18, but press blue clay into the rubber stamp and then apply the motif to a sheet of translucent. Apply the Sutton sheet to a sheet of white clay, then bake and quench.

APPLIQUÉ MOTIF

17 Clay cloisonné

Gold mica powder; ocher clay for background plus turquoise, violet and yellow for motif
How-to: Roll logs of clay for the floral motif and coat them in mica powder. Shape half of each log into a teardrop and then apply thin slices of the round and teardrop logs to the background clay (see page 111).

20 Rainbow Sutton

White and translucent clay plus a blend of translucent rainbow colors
How-to: Make this in the same way as tile 18, but press white clay into the rubber stamp and then apply the motif to a sheet of translucent. Apply the Sutton sheet to a blended sheet of translucent rainbow colors, then bake and quench.

SUTTON SLICE

18 Sutton flower

Brown and white clay
How-to: Press a sheet of white clay into a deeply etched rubber stamp, then use a tissue blade to slice off the excess clay (see page 110). Press the stamp onto a sheet of brown clay to transfer the motif, then roll flat.

21 Double Sutton

Brown, white and black clay
How-to: Make tile 18 and roll flat. Then press tile 18 into another rubber stamp (the one used here featured an all-over pattern of cracks). Repeat the Sutton slice technique to transfer the clay from the recesses in the second rubber stamp to a sheet of black clay, then roll flat.

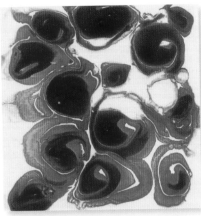

LIQUID CLAY

22 Random swirls

White and red oil paint and liquid clay; white clay

How-to: Using a small amount of oil paint, mix some white and red liquid clay. Paint a sheet of white polymer clay with white liquid clay and then add dots of red. Use a needle tool to draw spirals in the red, starting at the center of each dot. Add as many spirals as you like and then bake.

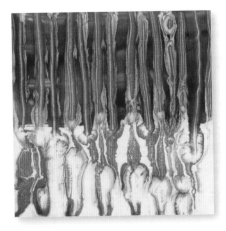

25 Thick dragged lines

White and red oil paint and liquid clay; white clay

How-to: Using a small amount of oil paint, mix some white and red liquid clay. Paint the top half of a sheet of white polymer clay with red liquid clay and the rest of the sheet with white liquid clay. Use a knitting needle to drag lines from the red section down through the white, wiping the needle after every use, and then bake.

23 Bleeding dots

White and black alcohol ink and liquid clay; white clay

How-to: Mix 6 drops of white ink into 1 tbsp (15ml) of liquid clay; repeat with black ink. Paint a sheet of white polymer clay with white liquid clay and then add dots of black. Leave for 30 minutes so that the black ink can bleed into the white and then bake. The bubbles are caused by the alcohol ink; use oil paint if you do not want any bubbling.

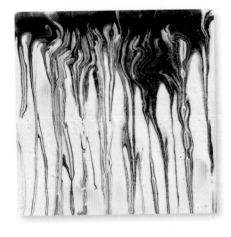

26 Thin dragged lines

White and black alcohol ink and liquid clay; white clay

How-to: Mix the colors as for tile 23. Continue as for tile 25, but only paint the black liquid clay along the top of the white polymer clay sheet and use a finer tool such as a toothpick.

24 Feathered stripes

White and red oil paint and liquid clay; champagne clay

How-to: Using a small amount of oil paint, mix some white and red liquid clay and apply in horizontal stripes across a sheet of champagne clay (see page 113). Use a knitting needle to drag vertical lines from top to bottom, then rotate the clay sheet 180 degrees and repeat. Bake the tile.

Tile by Alynne Landers.

27 Fine marbling

Colored liquid clay

How-to: A border of polymer clay is applied around the edges of a ceramic tile and then different colors of liquid clay are applied within the border in a very thin layer. A needle tool is used to swirl the colors to simulate the look of Italian marbled paper. After baking, the very thin sheet can be cut with scissors or a blade to the desired shape, or the sheet can be wrapped over an armature.

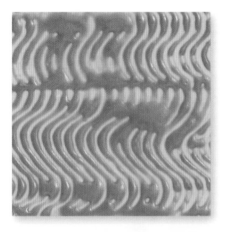

28 Combed squiggles
Brown and white oil paint and liquid clay; champagne clay
How-to: Mix a small amount of each oil paint into some liquid clay to create a beige color and then apply the mixture to a sheet of champagne clay. Use a rubber texture comb to drag a pattern of squiggly lines through the liquid clay and then bake (see page 113).

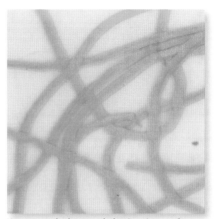

31 Golden threads
Gold, white and translucent clay
How-to: Extrude thin strings of gold clay as for tile 29 but this time lay the strings onto a thin sheet of translucent clay. Place a thin sheet of translucent on top to sandwich the strings. Use a roller to press the sheets together. Apply the whole thing to a sheet of white clay, roll again, then bake and quench.

You can apply the extruded strings in a random design, as here, or in a precise pattern.

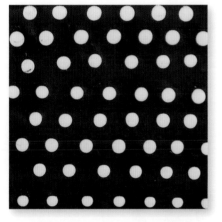

EXTRUSIONS

29 Polka dots
White and black clay
How-to: Extrude some thin strings of white clay and line them up on a ceramic tile (see page 106). Use a tissue blade to cut off small dots of white clay and apply them to a sheet of black clay. Roll together and then bake.

32 How long is a piece of string?
Gold clay
How-to: Extrude thin strings of clay and apply to a clay sheet in a pattern that you like (see page 107). Add tiny balls of clay between the strings if you wish, and use a needle tool and ball stylus to indent marks in some of the strings and balls.

30 Graphic stripes
White and black clay
How-to: Line up strings of extruded white clay as for tile 29. Place a sheet of black clay on top, roll lightly so that it sticks to the strings and then slide a tissue blade under the strings to release them from the ceramic tile (see page 106). Roll together and then bake.

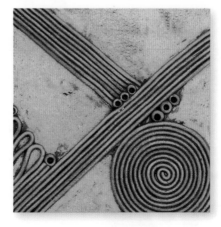

33 Antique coils
Brown acrylic paint; gold clay
How-to: Make this in the same way as tile 32, in any pattern you like, and then bake. When cool, apply a wash of acrylic paint, using a stencil brush to push the color into the indentations in the clay, then wipe off the excess with an old towel.

PATTERNS & MOTIFS

Polymer clay artists at work

The pieces displayed here showcase a wide variety of patterning techniques, from liquid clay applied in swirling layers of shimmering color to the holographic effects of mica shift ghost impressions. The beauty of these artworks is sure to inspire you to start experimenting with pattern effects, which is also a good incentive to expand your toolbox, from acquiring a selection of carving tools to an extruder with different die shapes for extruding different shapes of clay.

» See pages 114–119 for tile samples

▲ The memory of trees necklace
Martina Medenica
Techniques used: The focal pendant of this lovely beaded necklace features the ghost image of a tree in a Skinner blend of mica clay. This is embellished with beads on wires, some embedded directly onto the branches of the tree and others dangling below. The main pendant is 2¼ x 2in (5.5 x 5cm) and has been polished.
See MICA SHIFT tile 9

Circles in black and white necklace
Lynda Braunstein-Gilcher
Techniques used: This 18in (46cm) long necklace is stop-you-on-the-street drama. Disks of white clay cut out with a round cutter are decorated with black clay extrusions in dot, spiral and grid patterns. The patterned disks are alternated with textured and curved black disks. The largest disk is 1½in (4cm); the smallest is ¾in (2cm).
See EXTRUSIONS tiles 29–31

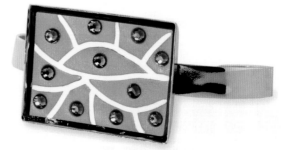

▲ Organic cell bangle
Anna Maria Gray
Techniques used: A 2½in (6.5cm) diameter brass bracelet blank is used to hold a 1 x 1¼in (2.5 x 3cm) rectangle of clay as the focal decorative piece. The colored clay is carved with a pattern of lines that are then backfilled with white clay, and Swarovski crystals are added between the pathways to accent the individual cells of the design. The piece was inspired by the process of cell division and how simple parts combine to create a complex whole.
See CARVING tile 14

▶ Mica ripple bead necklace
Carol Blackburn

Techniques used: This necklace looks dramatic but uses relatively simple techniques. Sheets of silver mica clay are stacked on top of each other, then the stack is set on its side and ⅛in (3mm) thick slices are cut with a ripple blade. The slices are run through a pasta machine several times to reduce the thickness by half, passing the clay through the machine with the ripple lines vertical each time. Triangles in two different sizes are cut from the flattened clay, curved slightly, pierced with a needle tool and then baked. The curved mica beads are threaded so that the curves face in alternate directions—a simple adjustment that has great design impact. The beads are about 2in (5cm) and 3in (7.5cm) long.
See MICA SHIFT tile 1

▼ Oil-painted bead necklace
Debbie Crothers

Techniques used: Three coats of liquid clay colored with oil paint or mixed with mica powder are dropped or painted onto solid-colored beads. The liquid clay is heat-set with a portable tool so that subsequent sections can be worked on without smudging previously embellished areas. The glossy finish and fluid swirling designs of the liquid clay combine to create a highly effective imitation of glass beads. The beads are about 1¼–1⅜in (3–3.5cm) long.
See LIQUID CLAY tile 22

◀ Feathered bangles
Carol Blackburn

Techniques used: Colored liquid clay is randomly painted and dragged with combs to create feathered patterns that look like fine marbling. The feathered sheets are then applied to black clay bangles that are 1½in (4cm) wide and 3¼in (8cm) diameter. The rich, shimmering colors of the feathered liquid clay effectively imitate silk-painted fabric.
See LIQUID CLAY tiles 24–27

▶ De Stijl earrings
Saskia Veltenaar

Techniques used: These earrings were inspired by the De Stijl artistic movement founded in the Netherlands, such as the paintings of Piet Mondrian and the furniture of Gerrit Rietveld. A wallpaper sample is used to texture the clay to give it the look of linen fabric. The block patterns are formed on 1¾ x ⅝in (4.5 x 1.5cm) rectangles of clay, and the earrings are finished with sterling silver findings. It is easier to build block patterns like these as large sheets from which you can cut out the shapes required. A brooch in this design would be equally effective.
See BLOCK PATTERNS tiles 12–13

...quid clay colored with pigment powders and alcohol ...ed together randomly to create a sheet veneer that can be cut ...he required size and shape to create pendants, earrings and brooches. The veneer is applied to a 2¼ x 3¾in (5.5 x 9.5cm) blue clay piece in the shape of a fan, and then coated with a clear medium for added shine.
See LIQUID CLAY tiles 22–27

▲ Mask
Debi L. Drew

Techniques used: This dramatic piece of extruded coilwork is a perfect example of the possibilities of the technique. Polymer clay has been pressed over a handbuilt ceramic clay form, and then decorated with extruded strings of polymer clay in curving and spiral patterns. The 5in (12.5cm) square mask is mounted onto an abstract painting.
See EXTRUSIONS tiles 32–33

▶ Treasure beads
Sharon Solly

Techniques used: Lots of different bead shapes are embellished with clear and colored liquid clays in a variety of patterns. Each liquid clay layer is heat-set before the next is applied. The liquid clay patterns give these beads wonderful texture as well as design panache, showcasing the beautiful effects that can be achieved with this medium. The finished beads look remarkably like glass lampwork beads, but without the extreme heat involved in their making.
See LIQUID CLAY tiles 22–23

◀ Carved light switch plate
Marie Segal

Techniques used: A 5 x 3in (12.5 x 7.5cm) metal light switch plate is covered with a sheet of black clay and then baked. When cool, a design is carved into the black clay and gold clay is pressed into the carved lines. Excess gold clay is scraped off with a ceramic clean-up tool, and then the piece is rebaked. The high-gloss finish is achieved entirely through sanding and buffing.
See CARVING tile 14

▶ Faux textile bangle

Lisa Pavelka

Techniques used: A wooden armature is covered with a faux textile effect created using a graduated Skinner blend of clay and a Sutton type technique. The inside of the bangle is covered with a strip of matte, heavily textured clay that contrasts with the shiny pattern of squiggly lines on the faces of the bangle. The 4in (10cm) square bracelet is accented with an edging of purple and white stripes.

See SUTTON SLICE tiles 18–20

▲ Spring beads

Sharon Solly

Techniques used: These beads are made in the same way as the treasure beads opposite, but using a pretty pastel color palette. Pastel colors can be created by mixing some white liquid clay with colored liquid clay. Alternatively, you can create pastel colors by mixing white and colored oil paints into clear liquid clay. Clear and colored Kato Liquid Polyclay was used for these beads (and those opposite) because it becomes shiny and glass-like when baked at a hot enough temperature.

See LIQUID CLAY tiles 22–23

◀ White flower pendant

Ponsawan Sila

Techniques used: A sheet of black polymer clay is added to an annealed steel wire frame and then baked. When cool, the clay is carved and backfilled with white clay. Notice that only some of the carved lines are filled—lines radiating outward at the bottom and to the right of the flower have been left unfilled to provide textural lines that echo the lines of the wirework. A handbuilt wire leaf is attached at the bottom of the frame to complete the 5 x 2½in (12.5 x 6.5cm) pendant.

See CARVING tile 14

◀ Pottery shard ornament

Marie Segal

Techniques used: The Sutton slice technique is used to create the blue-and-white patterned centerpiece. A round piece of the patterned clay is framed in a circular clay mount topped with a molded angel complete with halo. After baking, the piece is stained with brown acrylic paint and the excess wiped off. The patterned disk is then covered with UV resin to give the look of an old piece of Delftware porcelain made into a Christmas ornament— perfect as a gift for friends and family. The ornament measures 3½ x 3in (9 x 7.5cm).

See SUTTON SLICE tile 19

PAVÉ & MOSAIC

Pavé effects

The French word *pavé* means "paving stone" or "cobblestone," and is used in jewelry-making to refer to gemstones set close together so that the piece of jewelry looks as if it were paved in gemstones. Pavé-style effects can be created in polymer clay by covering the clay with an all-over embellishment or repeating pattern, from gluing on crystals to applying molded clay shapes.

You will need:

- Polymer clay, pasta machine (optional), roller and tissue blade
- Your choice of pavé embellishment:
  » Sand, chip stones or other small crushed stones
  » Flat-backed glass/crystal rhinestones, embellishment pick-up pencil (or similar) and heat-set glue with metal nozzle (such as fabric glitter glue)
  » JeJe peel-off stickers (or similar) and sharp scissors
  » Approx. 6ft (1.8m) length of ball chain (such as from a fan pull) and ceramic tile or Plexiglas sheet
  » Chain mold
  » Brass stencil of small leaves (or other motifs), round and teardrop cutters and paring knife

Queen bee brooch
Marie Segal
The heart-shaped background is embellished with an all-over pavé design of molded clay bees.

Encrusted sand

1 Protect your work surface with a piece of cardstock or cardboard, then pour out some sand (or crushed stone) and spread it in an even layer. Using the same color clay and sand will produce a lovely textured, sparkling surface, but combining different colors can also look good. White sand and white clay are used here.

2 Press a sheet of clay onto the sand. Move the clay around over the pile, pressing your fingers on the back of the clay to help the sand to stick. Be careful that you do not tear or distort the clay.

3 Turn over the clay and check to see if there is an even layer of sand all over it. If there are any gaps, place the clay back down on the sand and press sand onto the bare areas. Once the whole surface is fully covered, roll over the back of the clay to make sure that the sand is well pressed in. Be firm, but do not press too hard.

4 Take the clay off the pile of sand and turn it over on a clean area of your work surface. Gently roll over the front of the clay, forward and back. Turn the clay 90 degrees and roll forward and back again. When the sand is fully embedded, bake the encrusted clay.

Rhinestones

1 Place the metal nozzle onto the tip of the glue bottle, then squeeze two or three dots of glue along the top edge of the clay. Space the dots to suit the size of the stones you are using and the spacing you require. Here, the stones are being applied to a square sheet of clay in straight rows, but you can also apply them in a random design or in any pattern you like.

2 Press a pick-up pencil straight down onto a rhinestone and then lift it up. Place the stone onto the first dot of glue. Just place it lightly; you do not have to press the stone into the clay. Place the next stone in the same way, adjusting the spacing of the stones as required. Continue adding glue dots and rhinestones along the top edge of the clay.

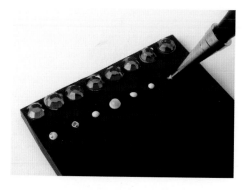

3 Add the next row of glue dots and rhinestones in the same way. Here, brown rhinestones are alternated with rows of contrasting white stones. If the contrasting stones are a different size from the first row (as here), position the first couple of stones to determine the correct spacing before completing the row. Otherwise, use the first row as a guide to spacing.

4 If the pick-up pencil stops sticking or gets dirty, rub it on a piece of paper or sharpen it just a little to make it work again. Continue adding rows of rhinestones. If you need to adjust the position of a stone, simply nudge it with the tip of the pencil. Keep checking alignment as you go because you need to make adjustments before the glue sets. Don't worry if any glue is visible because it will dry clear. Bake to cure the clay and set the glue.

Tips & techniques

■ Hot-fix crystals already have adhesive on the back. You can position the crystals onto raw clay and then bake, or apply them to baked clay and use a stone-setting heat tool to set the glue.

■ Use crystal or glass rhinestones when applying to raw clay so that you can bake them in the oven along with the clay. If gluing the crystals in place, choose a heat-set glue that will cure at the same time as you bake the clay. If you wish to use acrylic stones, bake the clay first and then glue on the stones with a suitable glue. Gluing stones to raw clay rather than baked clay is easier, though—the raw clay sort of "grabs" the stones.

■ If using stones with a pointed back, roll the clay thicker than the depth of the stones. Press each stone into the clay so that the widest edge of the stone is just below the surface; this small overlap of clay will hold the stones in place after baking without the need for gluing. You can use the new eraser on the end of a pencil or a rubber-tipped clay shaping tool to press in the stones.

■ The embellishment pick-up pencil has a sticky core instead of graphite and is ideal for picking up and placing stones onto clay. If you do not have one, put a little hand-softened beeswax or a stick-type glue (like rubber cement) onto the end of a toothpick or skewer.

■ If you find it difficult to keep rows of stones (or other pavé embellishments) straight, place a piece of cardstock under the first few stones to help you align the rest along the row. Alternatively, plot a grid on the clay as guidance; just mark the grid rather than piercing holes right through the clay (see page 147).

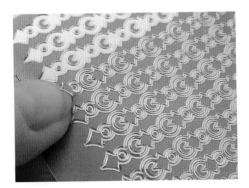

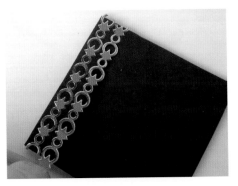

Peel-off stickers

1 Many of the stickers used by papercrafters and scrapbookers can be applied directly onto raw clay and then baked with the clay, although they may change slightly in appearance. Always do a test piece to check the suitability of your stickers. To peel off, bend the master sheet slightly and pry up a row of stickers with a thumbnail.

2 Roll out the clay and cut to the required size. Position a strip of stickers along the top edge, pressing gently into place with a fingertip. Trim off the excess with scissors. Keep adding strips of stickers, one at a time and trimming to fit. When the clay is covered, gently press the stickers down with your fingers or a roller to make sure that they are well attached.

3 When trimming the ends of each sticker row, leave the trimmed stickers on the scissors and transfer the leftover piece back onto the master sheet to save for another time. The little piece left here would be perfect as a watch hand, for example—nothing need be wasted in polymer clay. Bake the finished piece, then cover with resin if you wish.

Impressed dots

1 Roll out a sheet of clay slightly larger than required and use a tissue blade to trim the bottom edge straight. Starting at one end of a long length of ball chain, lay the chain across the bottom edge of the clay. Press the chain into the clay, taking care not to press any deeper than a quarter of the thickness of the clay.

2 Fold the chain back and forth over the clay, pressing the balls in gently as you go, up to the top of the clay. Lay a ceramic tile or sheet of Plexiglas on top of the chain and press down firmly. Depending on the softness of the clay, you may have to apply some force.

3 Remove the tile or Plexiglas and peel the chain off the clay. Trim the textured clay to the required size, looking for the nicest area of the piece you have made, and then bake. The finished look is like inverted cobblestones.

Molded chain

1 Buy a mold or make your own (see page 142). Here, putty silicone molding compound has been used to make a mold of a length of curb link chain from an old watch band. Roll a log of clay, slightly longer than the mold. The log should be thick enough to fill the mold, with just a little left over to trim off.

2 Press the log into the mold. Holding a tissue blade horizontally, slice off the excess clay above the surface of the mold. Try not to "saw" it off; instead, move the blade smoothly across the top of the mold in one fluid motion.

3 Holding the very end of the mold, gently pull out the clay. You may have to pick up the mold and bend it to help release the clay. Place the molded piece along one edge of the clay being decorated, allowing it to overlap at the sides. Gently press into place to tack it to the surface.

4 Cover the whole surface with chain-molded strips. If using soft clay or molded pieces that are not flat on top, trim each strip as you go, taking care not to distort the molded design. If using firmer clay and flat molded pieces, you can turn the whole piece over and trim from the back.

5 The chain used for this mold is curbed, so the links are flat on top and the piece can be turned over. Holding the blade against each edge, cut straight down and then move the blade outward without lifting it. Bake the finished piece.

Quick molded pavé

Make a mold of your finished pavé design so that you can replicate it quickly and easily.

Choosing a mold

Commercial molds are available in a huge range of designs, but it is easy to make your own using polymer clay or putty silicone. Thicker, stiffer molds work best for this technique, so that the mold will hold its shape when you press clay into it. If you only have a more flexible molding compound, make the mold thicker on the back and sides. Alternatively, make a polymer clay support to hold the mold when you press in the clay. Molded chain is a quick way to create pavé designs, because you only have to apply a few strips but get the effect of lots of links. Molds of novelty buttons and charms also work well, though each piece has to be molded and applied individually.

Stenciled leaves

1 Roll out some clay, ⅛in (3mm) thick, then fold in half to double the thickness. Here, the same color clay is used for the leaves and background piece, but you can use contrasting colors if you prefer. Cut out several disks of clay using a round cutter and roll them into balls; you will probably have to cut out more as you go, depending on the size of your project. Flatten the balls slightly and roll some of them into logs. A ½in (13mm) cutter and ½in (13mm) long logs are suitable for most of the leaves on the stencils used here; adjust the sizes to suit your stencil as necessary.

2 Place different leaf shapes over the balls and logs of clay to check what size and shape of clay will best fit the stencil. Use balls for leaf shapes that are roughly equal in width and length; use logs for longer leaves.

3 Place the leaf stencil over the ball or log of clay. Use a fingernail or a tool such as the tip of a paring knife (see step 5) to press down the edge of the stencil around the shape. The aim is to push the clay up through the center of the stencil pattern and produce a domed leaf shape.

Choosing a stencil

A basic brass stencil with simple one-piece shapes is the best choice for this technique. All of the leaves on both of these stencils are suitable. Multi-piece designs such as the berry on the smaller stencil can be used, but they are harder to work with as they tend to fall apart when sliced off. The little stems that hold the berries are fun to use, though.

4 Holding a tissue blade flat on the stencil, slice off the leaf with a slight sawing motion. Gently work your way around the leaf to slice it free. If the blade catches under an edge of the stencil, saw back out and then slice from a different place or angle to cut the leaf free. Place the leaf on the piece of clay being decorated, pressing it on gently.

5 Continue adding leaves one at a time to the background piece, working systematically along one edge. If you are using firmer clay, it will be harder to press through the stencil but easier to slice off. Softer clay will push through easily but be harder to slice off. My preference is for firmer clay and a leaf that is easier to slice off.

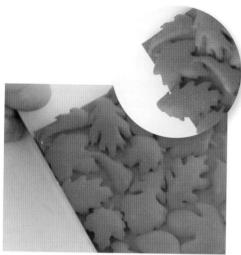

6 Continue building up the "cobblestone" leaf pattern using a variety of stencil shapes. If any of the clay leaves do not come out very well, add them to your scrap pile and start again. If a leaf overhangs the edge, trim it and use the trimmed section to fill a gap along another edge. Gently press all of the leaves to attach them to the surface below. When finished, trim away any excess from the sides.

7 Mark the veins on the leaves. Use a knife to mark the center vein, dragging the tip of the blade along the surface of the leaf. Mark the vein clearly but take care not to cut through the leaf.

8 The quickest way to mark the side veins is to use a teardrop cutter because you can mark pairs of veins at the same time, but take care to position the point of the cutter into the center vein and to keep the round end raised above the clay.

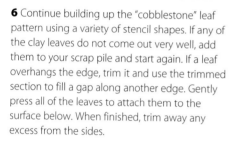

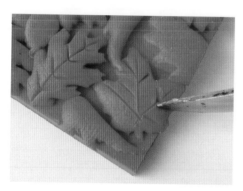

9 For variety, use the knife blade to mark non-symmetrical side veins on some of the leaves. Continue marking all of the veins, taking care to mark them clearly but not cut too deeply. Bake the finished piece.

Adding color
Stain the leaf with acrylic paint and then add metallic highlights (see page 32).

Cane and cutter slices

Thin slices of decorative canes or shapes cut out using a small cutter can be applied to a clay background to create a pavé pattern. Place all of the slices onto the clay lightly; do not press them down until they are all in place in case you need to adjust the spacing. Go over the edges of the clay to complete the pattern if necessary, letting the slices overhang. Once the pattern is complete, trim off the excess; ideally, turn the piece over and trim from the back because this is less likely to cause cracking. If you wish, roll the slices into the clay slightly using a roller over the front.

PAVÉ & MOSAIC

Mosaic designs

It is easy to create mosaics in polymer clay. When working with baked clay, you can glue clay tesserae in place just as you would with a ceramic mosaic. When working with raw clay, the mosaic pieces will stick to the clay beneath or you can inlay them. Polymer clay mosaics can be grouted like a traditional mosaic.

You will need:

- Pasta machine, roller and tissue blade

- Non-sanded tile grout and small squeegee

- Polymer clay in brown, white and black for snail spiral mosaic

- Black polymer clay, faux shell cane in a basketweave pattern (see page 82) and sharp scissors for shell mosaic

- Polymer clay in any colors you like, selection of small cutters and texture stick or similar tool (see page 54) for cutter mosaic

Mosaic cat brooch
Lilian Nichols
The cat is formed from brightly colored strips of clay that are then divided into smaller pieces with a craft knife. The grouting is polymer clay mixed with a little mineral oil.

Snail spiral mosaic
1 Roll out sheets of black, white and brown clay, ⅛in (3mm) thick, and make a Skinner blend using half triangles of black and brown with a full triangle of white in between (see pages 20–21). The template for the blend should measure 8 x 1½in (20 x 4cm).

2 Use a tissue blade to straighten the edges of the blended strip. Cut sections off the end of the strip, holding the blade at an angle. Each section should be about ¼in (6mm) on one side and ⅛in (3mm) on the other. Alternate the angle at which you hold the blade, so that alternating sections have wider black and brown edges.

3 Curve the triangular sections into flat spirals and place them onto a sheet of clay, alternating colors. A square tile of white clay left over from making the Skinner blend is used here, but the color is not important because it will be covered with grout.

4 Cover the clay with the spirals, overlapping the edges if there is not enough room for a full spiral. Turn the tile over and trim off the excess spirals from the back, cutting straight down with the blade and then moving the blade outward without lifting it. Bake and allow to cool, then apply grout to the finished piece (see page 133).

Shell mosaic light switch plate
Marie Segal
Mosaic pieces cut from several faux shell canes in different colors are applied to black clay over a metal switch plate.

Shell mosaic

1 Cut off a slice of clay from the faux shell cane, roll it out very thinly—about 1/32in (1mm)—and bake. Plan your design. Think in mosaic shapes and keep it simple if you want it to look like a real shell mosaic. If you draw the plan on paper, you can cut out templates for the various mosaic shapes.

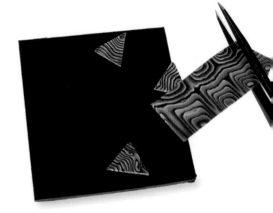

2 Using very sharp scissors, start to cut out the mosaic pieces. If you are taking a freeform approach rather than using templates, start by cutting a strip of clay and then divide this into triangles. They will all be slightly different from each other, but this can be very effective in some designs.

3 Roll out a sheet of clay to form the background for your mosaic design. This mosaic will be inlaid into the clay with no grouting, so choose a color that will show off the mosaic pieces to best effect. Black works particularly well for this faux shell, which has black striations running through it. Press the pieces onto the clay in the required pattern.

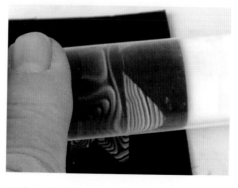

4 When all of the pieces are in place, use a roller to push them into the clay sheet so that the surface of the mosaic pieces is level with the surrounding clay.

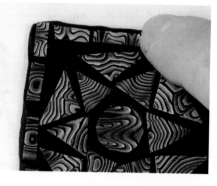

5 Adding a simple border around a central motif can look very effective in a mosaic design. When you are happy with the result, bake the finished piece.

Every slice of faux shell cane will be slightly different, and each side of every slice will be different as well, so spend some time choosing which parts of the cane will best suit your mosaic design.

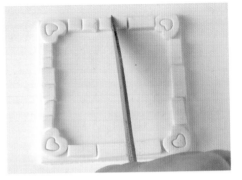

Cutter mosaic

1 Roll out a sheet of clay, ⅛in (3mm) thick, and cut out a 2in (5cm) square tile to decorate with the mosaic (or whatever shape and size piece you wish). Use the leftover clay sheet and a small cutter to cut out a mosaic piece for each corner of the tile. A ⅜in (1cm) heart cutter is used here. Press the hearts onto the corners, points outward.

2 Use a smaller ³⁄₁₆in (4.5mm) cutter to impress a heart in the middle of each of the corner hearts. This will fill with grout and look like there are two hearts placed there.

3 Cut ⅛in (3mm) wide strips from the clay sheet and cut them into ¼in (6mm) sections. Place these around the edges of the tile, starting in the center of each edge and then filling in the rest of the spaces. Cut to fit where necessary. If you do not like the look of the long pieces (as here), use a blade to divide them into smaller pieces.

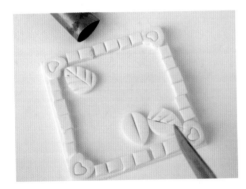

4 Use a ½in (13mm) teardrop cutter to cut out three leaves and place them on the tile. Use a blade to mark the leaf veins. Don't cut through the leaves; just make deep marks in the clay.

5 Use a ¾in (2cm) flower cutter to cut out two flowers. Push the clay shapes out of the cutter with a finger and turn them over so that the flat side is face up. Cut out the center of each flower with a ⅜in (1cm) round cutter.

6 Position the flowers on the tile; here, one whole and one half flower have been used. Cut out ³⁄₁₆in (5mm) circles of clay and cut one in half. Place them smooth side up in the center of the flowers.

If using a cutter with a plunger for easy removal of the cutout shape, the plunger will leave a dimple in the clay, so place the dimpled side face down.

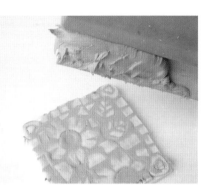

7 Mark the little circles with a texture stick (see page 54) or simply indent them with a round mark using a ball stylus or similar tool.

8 Cut some strips of clay, about ³⁄₁₆in (4.5mm) wide, and cut them into random shapes and sizes. Use them to fill in the background of the tile. Mark the pieces with a blade if any look too large or too close together. Mark lines to indicate petals on the flowers. Bake the tile and allow to cool completely.

9 Squeeze a blob of grout onto the baked tile and use a squeegee to spread the grout into all the spaces and crevices. Scrape off the excess grout, let it sit for about an hour and then use wet fingers to wipe off any remaining excess grout.

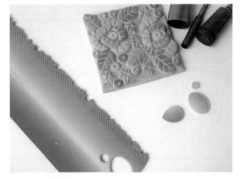

Shape variations
You do not have to make a square tile using this technique. You can add a border around the mosaic pieces and cut out the shape to make a brooch or pendant. Try covering a ball of clay and piercing it to make a bead. This is a wonderful technique for covering all sorts of vessels and objects.

10 Allow the grout to set overnight, then polish the tile with a damp piece of old towel. Notice how the little texture marks in the center of the flowers now show through the grout. It is normal for the grout to darken after setting, so choose the color carefully. The grayish blue grout used here works well with the white clay mosaic.

Blended cutter mosaic
Try using a color blend to make a cutter mosaic; this blend is the same as the snail spiral blend on page 130, but using green, white and pink. Vary the placement of the cutters to get different shades of color. The rose petals are made from ovals cut in half, and all markings on the leaves and roses are made with a blade. The rose centers are indented with a ball stylus.

PAVÉ & MOSAIC

Tile samples

Jewelers use the word pavé to refer to a covering of close-set gemstones, but artists working in polymer clay can think in broader terms when exploring this versatile material's huge potential. Remember that pavé literally means cobblestone or paving, and there are countless ways of decoratively "paving" a polymer clay piece. An all-over covering of beads, stones or crystals can look spectacular, but so too can molded or stenciled clay shapes. Pavé embellishments can be applied randomly or in a regular pattern across the whole surface of the clay beneath, but you can also use them to create mosaic designs or diaper patterns (small repeated units that connect or interlock).

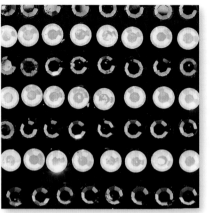

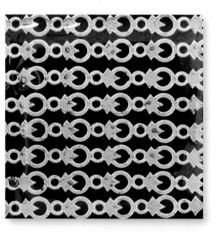

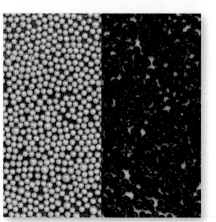

Pearl pink beads on sapphire blue clay (left) and black glitter beads on white clay (right).

Zigzag pendant
Lilian Nichols

Strips of different-colored clays are laid side by side to make a striped sheet. Strips are then cut from the sheet and applied in offset rows to create a tile pattern of zigzagging colors.

JEWELED PAVÉ

1 Rhinestone cowboy
Flat-backed glass or crystal rhinestones and heat-set glue; bronze clay (2 parts black/ 1 part gold)
How-to: Roll out clay, apply dots of glue, place a rhinestone onto each glue dot and then bake (see page 125).

2 Tick tock
JeJe peel-off stickers and UV resin; bronze clay (2 parts black/1 part gold)
How-to: Apply stickers to raw clay (see page 126). You can apply the stickers in rows, as here, or in a more random design, depending on the sticker design you are using. Bake, allow to cool and then coat with resin.

3 Seed beads
Hole-less pink and black glass seed beads and heat-set glue; sapphire blue and white clay
How-to: Pour some beads onto a paper plate. Roll out the clay and cover with glue, then place the clay, glue side down, on top of the beads. Press gently on the raw clay and move it around in the beads so that the whole surface is covered (add more beads to the plate if necessary), then bake.

ENCRUSTED EFFECTS

4 Sparkling sand

White sand; white clay mixed with tiny amount of magenta clay

How-to: Spread out a pile of sand, press sheet of clay onto it, roll over the clay with a roller to press the sand into the surface and then bake (see page 124).

5 Blacktop

Activated charcoal; black clay

How-to: Impress the charcoal into the clay as for tile 4. The result simulates encrusted jet or the appearance of blacktop. Pressing a stencil brush straight up and down onto the clay or pressing coarse sandpaper into the clay surface also creates a blacktop texture but without the sparkle (see page 50).

PRINTED PAVÉ

6 Sweethearts

Red silk screen paint; black clay

How-to: Use heart-shaped sequin scrap to screen print multiple hearts onto a sheet of clay (see page 70). Sequin scrap is the leftover material after the sequins have been punched out and comes in lots of different designs and sizes.

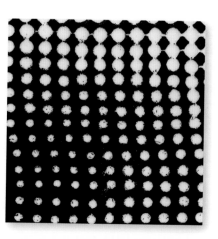

7 Dot to dot

Black ink pad; white clay

How-to: Use a length of ball chain to impress dots into a sheet of clay (see page 126). Tap an ink pad onto the clay until the surface is covered with ink and then bake. The impressed dots will remain visible where the ink could not reach.

SHAPED CLAY

8 Golden leaves

Ocher clay

How-to: Use a brass leaf stencil to make a variety of small leaf shapes, apply them to a sheet of clay in a random design, mark veins on the leaves and then bake (see page 128).

9 Midnight leaves

Turquoise and copper acrylic paint; black clay

How-to: Make and bake in the same way as tile 8. When cool, apply a wash of turquoise acrylic, using a stencil brush to push the color into the indentations in the clay, then wipe off the excess (see page 32). Use a fingertip to brush on metallic copper highlights.

See page 40 for alternative colorway.

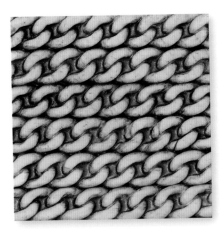

10 Chain gang
Bronze acrylic paint; white clay
How-to: Make a mold of a length of chain or use a ready-made mold. Form strips of clay in the mold, lay them across a clay sheet and then bake (see page 127). When cool, apply a wash of acrylic paint, making sure that it goes into all of the indentations in the clay, then wipe off the excess.

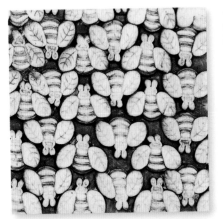

11 Busy bees
Brown acrylic paint; white clay
How-to: Make a mold of a bee (this one was made from a novelty button) or use a ready-made mold. Apply molded clay bees to a sheet of clay. Here, columns of bees alternately face upward and downward, with their wings interlocking. Bake and color with acrylic paint (as tile 10).

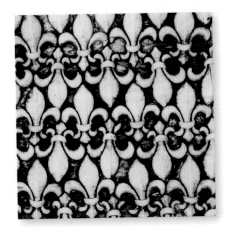

12 Fleur de lis
Black acrylic paint; white clay
How-to: Make a mold of a fleur de lis (this one was made from a bracelet charm) or use a ready-made mold. Apply molded shapes to a sheet of clay. Here, staggered rows of fleur de lis alternately point upward and downward. Bake and color with acrylic paint (as tile 10).

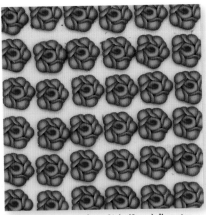

Reduce the cane to about ⁵/₁₆in (8mm) diameter (see page 81) before slicing.

CANE & CUTTER SLICES

13 Rose garden
Small-diameter cane; white clay
How-to: Apply thin slices of cane, evenly spaced, onto a sheet of white clay, then bake. This rose cane is made using a blended sheet of pink and white clay, rolled up into a log with white on the inside. Sections of the log are flattened, reshaped or rerolled and then combined to form a rose cane.

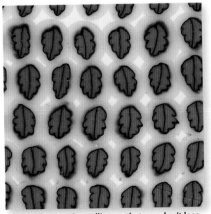

Reduce the cane by pulling so that you don't lose the indentations (see page 81).

14 Leaf fall
Small-diameter cane; white clay
How-to: Lay thin slices of cane onto a sheet of white clay. Use a roller to press the cane slices into the background clay and then bake. This leaf cane is a log of pink clay wrapped in a thin sheet of black; halve the cane, insert a sliver of black, join the two halves and indent the edges.

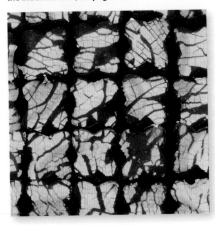

15 Golden lilacs
Gold leaf; translucent and black clay
How-to: Roll out translucent clay as thinly as possible. Apply gold leaf (see page 34) and use a roller to spread the leaf a little. Cut out shapes with a cutter; a ½in (13mm) lilac flower cutter is used here. Place gold side down onto a sheet of black clay. Roll the shapes into the clay, then bake and quench.

BEAD MOSAIC

16 Star mosaic

Multicolored glass seed beads; translucent and liquid clay
How-to: Roll out translucent clay and place seed beads onto the clay, one at a time, with a needle tool. The brightly colored beads are used here to create a symmetrical starburst design. Cover with liquid clay and then bake.

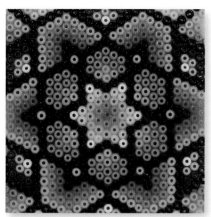

Tile by Tina Goodrich.

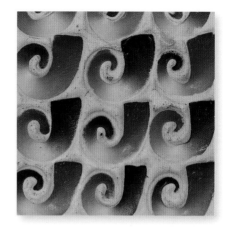

19 Snail spirals

Grout; black, white and brown clay
How-to: Make a three-color blended strip of clay, slice off triangular sections and coil into spiral shapes. Apply the spirals to a sheet of white clay and then bake (see page 130). Grout the finished tile.

17 Sunburst mosaic

Multicolored glass seed beads; translucent and liquid clay
How-to: Make and bake in the same way as tile 16. Here, the bead design is arranged asymmetrically, as if radiating outward from the top left corner. Try sketching out designs in colored pencil first and then use two L-shaped pieces of cardboard to test different crops.

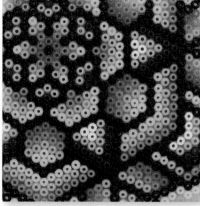

Tile by Tina Goodrich.

20 Monochrome cutter mosaic

Grout; white clay
How-to: Roll out the white clay and use cutters and a blade to cut out different shapes (see page 132). Apply them to a sheet of white clay and then bake. Grout the finished tile.

CLAY MOSAIC

18 Shell mosaic

Faux shell cane in a basketweave pattern (see page 82); black clay
How-to: Use sharp scissors to cut out mosaic pieces from a thin baked slice of faux shell cane. Apply pieces to a sheet of raw black clay, use a roller to inlay the mosaic and then bake (see page 131).

21 Blended cutter mosaic

Grout; green, white and pink clay
How-to: Make this in the same way as tile 20 but using a blended strip of clay (see page 133). Cut out the shapes to make the most of the shaded colors.

PAVÉ & MOSAIC

Polymer clay artists at work

Mosaic and pavé techniques are beautifully displayed and explored in the work of these polymer clay artists. The variations that are possible with these techniques can be seen in how the artists have played with similar elements to create very different results, from varying the size of mosaic pieces and whether or not grout is used to different ways of shaping clay to form pavé embellishments and using beads and crystals to complement both pavé and mosaic designs.

» See pages 134–137 for tile samples

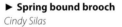

◀ **Mosaic beads**

Pavla Čepelíková

Techniques used: Colored sections of clay are applied to a hollow bead core and then marked with a blade to form small mosaic pieces that look like traditional ceramic mosaic tiles. The beads are grouted with gray polymer clay and then baked. Each bead is about 1¼in (3cm) diameter.

See CLAY MOSAIC tiles 19–21

▶ **Spring bound brooch**

Cindy Silas

Techniques used: Tiny strings of baked clay form the mosaic pieces in this pictorial design, with the colors and orientation of the strings being used to great effect in this lively landscape. The fields are dotted with slices of tiny bull's-eye canes for flowers and a slice of white log forms the rabbit's tail. No grouting is used. The piece is set in a 1¾in (4.5cm) diameter silver metal clay bezel textured with a commercial stamp.

See CLAY MOSAIC tiles 18–21

▲ **Canned world necklace**

Anna Maria Gray

This 24in (60cm) long necklace arose from the artist's concern over ecological disasters and the need to preserve the natural world. Various clay and bead micromosaic techniques are used to create the individual sections. The bead mosaics and detachable focal piece are placed within miniature frames of decorative clay. The two tin containers are lined with metal leaf to reflect light onto the mosaics within.

See BEAD MOSAIC tiles 16–17 and CLAY MOSAIC tiles 18–21

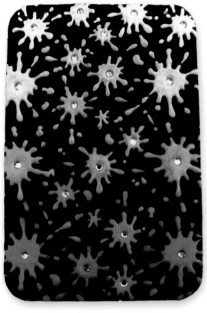

Colors of fall pavé necklace

Vera Kleist

Techniques used: Small balls of clay in graduated colors are applied to tube bead cores to create a pavé dragonskin effect. The clay colors are mixed with metallic clay containing mica particles to provide a subtle sparkle, which is enhanced by adding translucent clay to the mixture. The beads are strung together so that the fall colors graduate around the necklace. The closure is hidden in one of the beads. Each bead is about 1¼in (3cm) long and ⅜in (1cm) diameter.

See SHAPED CLAY tiles 11–12 (using balls of clay in place of molded pieces)

◀ **Sutton splat treasure tin**

Lisa Pavelka

Techniques used: A blended sheet of pink clay is applied to a sheet of black clay using a texture stamp with a splat motif and the Sutton slice technique (see page 110). The pink blend is applied to the stamp so that the color graduates from dark splats at the bottom to light at the top. The clay is used to cover a 3¾ x 2⅜in (9.5 x 6cm) metal tin and Swarovski hot-fix crystals are embedded into each raised splat to complement the pavé design.

See JEWELED PAVÉ tile 1 and SHAPED CLAY tiles 10–12 (using a texture sheet in place of a mold)

◀ **Tinachol box**

Tina Goodrich

Techniques used: Glass seed beads are applied to a sheet of polymer clay, then covered with liquid clay and baked. The mosaic sheet is then glued to the top of a wooden box measuring about 5¼in (13cm) square and 2½in (6.5cm) deep. The bead design is influenced by the art of Huichol Indians from central Mexico.

See BEAD MOSAIC tiles 16–17

◀ **Pavé slipper ornaments**

Nancy Nearing

Techniques used: A pattern for doll slippers was adapted for working with polymer clay, using two-layer sheets of clay to cut out both the inner and outer "fabric" of the slippers at the same time. The center slipper is made with metallic gold clay on the outside; the ecru-colored slippers on the left and right are silk screen printed with gold acrylic (see page 70). All three slippers are embellished with crystals to create a sparkling pavé ornament. Each slipper has a hanging loop to which a ribbon can be attached. The slippers are about 2¾in (7.5cm) long, 1½in (3.5cm) at the widest point on the sole and just over 1in (2.5cm) high at the heel (excluding hanging loop).

See JEWELED PAVÉ tile 1

EMBELLISHMENTS

Applied clay

Applying decorative clay shapes to another piece of clay is relatively easy to do because unbaked polymer clay sticks to itself easily. The pieces will remain securely joined as long as there is enough clay-to-clay contact. It is easy to make clay decorations using cutters, molds and simple sculpting techniques.

You will need:

- Polymer clay in the colors of your choice
- Pasta machine or roller, tissue blade and craft knife
- Selection of cutters (teardrop and round are used here) and large ball stylus
- Original piece to be molded (such as a charm), two-part putty silicone molding compound and measuring spoons

Using cutters

1 Roll out some clay, ⅛in (3mm) thick, and cut out a 2in (5cm) square tile. Use a teardrop cutter to cut out a leaf and press it onto the tile. Mark the center vein with a blade, then use the pointed end of the cutter to mark pairs of side veins. Raise the rounded end of the cutter so that only the pointed end marks the clay.

2 Alternatively, make a leaf by hand. Roll a ½in (13mm) ball of clay, shape it into a teardrop and then flatten slightly with your fingers. Press the leaf onto the tile in the desired position. Use a blade to mark the center vein and then the side veins.

3 Use a teardrop cutter to cut out the petals. A cutter with a more rounded shape is used here.

4 Start marking a decorative pattern onto the petals. Here, a scalloped flower cutter is used to mark across the widest part of each petal. This particular cutter is double-sided, with a pointed five-petal design on the top and a scalloped flower on the other side.

Wealth shrine brooch

Marie Segal

The basic house shape is embellished with decorative clay shapes, including logs and flattened balls as well as shapes cut out using small cutters—triangles, hearts and stars. The word at the base is molded.

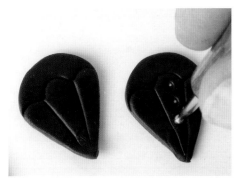

5 Use a blade to mark vertical lines from the base of each scallop to the pointed end of the petal. Make the lines deep but take care not to cut through the clay. Using a large ball stylus, indent a line of dots down the center section of each petal.

6 Bend each petal over your finger to shape it with a gentle curve, then add the petal to the tile. When all of the petals have been added, press in the center of the petals to attach them to the tile.

7 Roll a ¼in (6mm) ball of clay and flatten it between your thumb and forefinger. Press the flattened ball onto the middle of the petals. Use a small round cutter to mark a circle in the center.

8 Use the tip of a craft knife or small paring knife to mark lines around the edge of the center circle. Bake and then decorate as desired. The indented pattern on the flower and leaves provide well-defined sections for embellishing with glitter (see page 30).

Do you need to use glue?

There are several options for making strong attachments between pieces of polymer clay. However, every type of clay is slightly different, and the attachment method you choose will depend on what exactly you are trying to achieve and the finished use of the piece. There is no substitute for testing your materials. When gluing baked pieces together, clean the surfaces first with a cotton swab dipped in alcohol.

- Raw clay to raw clay: Simply press the clays together well. However, if the clay you are using is dry, lightly score the pieces where they are to be joined, apply some liquid clay or PVA glue and press together. If the clay is brittle after baking, add liquid clay or PVA glue to strengthen the joins and then rebake.

- Raw clay to baked clay: Lightly score the pieces and attach with liquid clay or PVA glue as above. Sometimes you can press raw clay onto baked clay, blend the join firmly, let the piece sit for a couple of days and then rebake; however, a thin layer of liquid clay or PVA glue will help the process and make a better attachment.

- Baked clay to baked clay: Attach the pieces together using PVA glue, liquid clay or epoxy glue; in each case, you will need to secure the pieces together until baked. Superglue also works very well and can be applied quite thinly to the clay and still hold; it will also bond straight away most of the time. Do not rebake the clay after using epoxy glue or superglue.

- Objects can be attached to polymer clay by embedding them in the clay or in a layer of liquid clay or melted wax (see pages 144–147). You can also glue objects to clay using PVA glue, superglue or epoxy glue (see page 12 for more information about glues).

Molding

1 Molds are an easy way of making clay decorations, and you can also make a mold of your finished work to speed up your production process. You can make molds in polymer clay, but the advantages of using two-part putty silicone molding compound are that the flexibility of the mold makes undercuts less of a problem and that you do not need to use a release agent. Mix together the two parts of the compound (see page 52)—⅛ tsp (0.5ml) of each is enough to make a mold of this ½in (13mm) fleur de lis charm; 1 tbsp (15ml) of each would be sufficient to make a mold of a 2in (5cm) square tile.

2 Roll a ball of the mixed compound and press it down over the charm, smoothing it around the edges to make sure that the whole charm is covered. Put the mold aside to set, as instructed on the package. When it is set, bend back the edge of the mold and the charm should pop free.

Heart of rock'n'roll pendant
Marie Segal
This pendant is a combination of handmade and molded pieces. The finished pendant can be molded for quick replication, and then new pendants made from the mold can be individualized with small alterations.

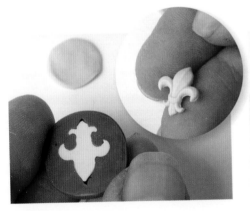

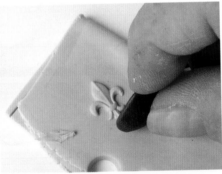

3 Roll a ball of clay, a little larger than the cavity, and press it firmly into the mold. If your mold has a deep recess, such as the nose on a face, roll the ball into a teardrop and place the point of the teardrop into the deep part of the mold. Slide a tissue blade across the surface of the mold to cut off the excess clay. Hold the mold by its edges and use a finger to press the back of the mold upward to release the clay.

4 Another way to release the molded piece is to press the filled mold down onto a thick sheet of clay. Lift up the edge of the mold and remove it; the molded piece should stay on the clay sheet. You can then slice the piece from the sheet of clay with a tissue blade.

5 A third method is to roll a small log of clay, flatten the end and press this onto the back of the piece in the mold to pull it free. Use a tissue blade to slice the molded piece off the clay plug.

Simple shapes like teardrops are easy to make, and are a good starting point for practicing your sculpting skills.

Handmade shapes

1 Roll five ¾in (2cm) balls of clay and shape them into 1–1¼in (2.5–3cm) long teardrops. Arrange them like a starfish. Place some screen mesh over them and cup your palm over the screen. This will texture the clay and your cupped hand will leave the center raised and the points flatter. Roll five smaller teardrops and apply them along each point of the starfish.

Charm bracelet
Marie Segal

Many pieces come together in this charm bracelet, from cane slices to sculpted pieces such as the rose below. The green leaves are simply balls of clay shaped into teardrops, then pressed flat and marked with lines for the veins (see page 140). Do not mark the lines too deeply or the leaves may break.

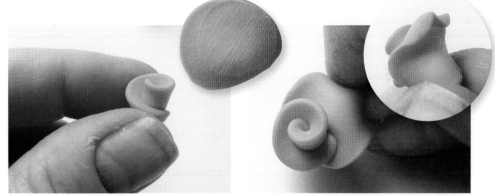

2 Use a blade to impress a deep line along each teardrop—just mark the lines; do not cut through the teardrops. This will ensure that the teardrops are stuck to the clay below and add extra textural interest. Take care not to mark any other parts of the clay when adding the lines. Stiff pieces of paper, old credit cards and paring knives are other useful marking tools.

Sculpted rose

1 Mix a Skinner blend shading from pink to white (see page 20), then roll out a long strip of the blended clay (see page 23). Roll up the strip to form a spiral cane with white in the center, then reduce to ¾in (2cm) thick (see pages 80–81). Cut off a ¹⁄₁₆in (1.5mm) thick slice and pinch one side to form a teardrop. Starting at the thicker end, roll up the teardrop to form the center of the rose.

2 Cut another slice of the cane; this time leave it round but press it to flatten it out. Apply it around the base of the rose center, allowing the slice to curve outward at the top. Pinch the center top of the petal to create a fluted edge. Continue adding more petals in this way.

EMBELLISHMENTS

Mixed media

This section shows several methods of adding a variety of objects and materials to polymer clay. There are many different options but these should give you a good foundation on which to build. Experiment to find ways that will work best for the particular piece you are making.

You will need:

- Polymer clay, pasta machine or roller and tissue blade
- Objects for embedding, such as chains, charms and beads, plus headpins and jump rings as attachment points
- Items for applying to surface, such as fabric, printed paper napkins and small clay shapes
- Encaustic wax medium (pre-made and mixed), hot plate and coffee can or melting pot, tweezers, tongue depressor and heat gun
- Liquid clay, mineral oil, mixing cup, paintbrush and denatured alcohol (for cleaning brush)
- Graph or grid paper, sharp needle and tiny hand drill
- Pliers, wire cutters and Teflon-coated scissors

Ball chains, eye screws and split rings can be embedded into the clay and then used as attachment points for other embellishments.

Embedding objects

1 Roll a sheet of clay, ⅛in (3mm) thick, and cut out a 2in (5cm) square tile. Place a ball chain over the edge of the tile. The closure will be covered here, but you can position it the other way around if you want to be able to open and close it. Cover it with another piece of clay. You can add a small amount of liquid clay or PVA glue, but it should not be necessary (see page 141).

2 Press the clay into place over the ball chain. Make sure that the clay is pressed well down all around the chain and where the chain protrudes from the clay at the top.

3 Use the same technique to embed eye screws and split rings. Make sure that at least half of the ring is exposed above the edge, adjusting the position if necessary. If the space is too small, it will be harder to attach things to them later.

Drop in a strange dream focal bead

Daniela D'Uva

A glass drop is encased in a handmade bezel of polymer clay and embellished with cane slices, thin logs of colored clay and tiny beads.

4 To add a bead so that it sits on the surface of the clay, thread the bead onto a headpin and use pliers to turn a loop next to the bead (needle-nose or rosary pliers are ideal for this). Trim the end of the wire just after the loop. Press the loop into the clay until the bead touches the clay. Press the clay tightly together around the loop.

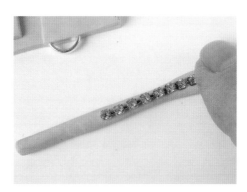

Arabian nights earrings
Marie Segal

Handmade wire rings are sandwiched between two strips of clay, with half of each ring embedded between the strips. Earwires are attached to the rings for wearing. See tile 5 on page 57 for how to make the decorative strips of clay used for the front of the earrings.

5 To embed a length of rhinestone or other decorative chain, roll a log of clay of about the same diameter as the chain. Press the chain into the log. Push the clay together around the chain and then press down again so that it is fully embedded. Press the log onto the tile.

6 Another way to attach a length of chain is to press the chain directly onto the clay tile. Press a small ball of clay onto each end of the chain to secure it in place. Try indenting the balls with a texture stick (see page 54) for additional decoration.

7 Press a glass donut bead onto the clay tile. You can put a small amount of PVA glue on the bottom of the glass for extra security if you wish. Roll four small balls of clay and shape them into teardrops. Place the teardrops over the donut bead. Press the outer ends of the teardrops into the clay on the outside of the bead.

8 To add a rhinestone to the center of the donut bead, roll a small ball of clay to suit the size of the stone. Press the stone into the ball and then bring up the sides of the clay around the stone. Press the stone into place on the donut bead so that the rhinestone setting is well attached to the four clay teardrops.

9 To add a flatbacked charm, thread the charm onto a jump ring and then press the jump ring into the clay. Press the clay together around the ring and use a knitting needle (or similar tool) to smooth the clay through the center of the ring. If the charm has no hanging loop, put a drop of PVA glue onto the back of the charm and press it onto the clay.

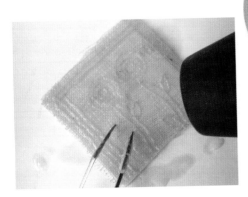

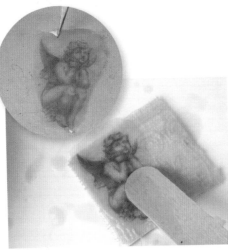

Encaustic wax

1 Work with baked clay when using encaustic wax. Melt some of the pellets of wax and use tweezers to immerse a piece of lace fabric in the melted wax. Place the waxed lace onto the clay. The lace will set on the clay as the wax cools. Use a heat gun if you need to reposition the lace, but keep the gun at least 6in (15cm) away from the surface.

2 Select a paper napkin with a printed design and separate the top printed layer. Cut out an image or two. Dip the cutout image into the hot wax, making sure that it is completely covered. Lay the image onto the lace and use a tongue depressor to flatten it out. Do this quickly or the stick will get stuck in the wax as it cools.

3 Try adding polymer clay embellishments, such as shapes cut out of a very thin sheet of clay using paper punches or cutters. Hold each shape on the decorated surface and use the heat gun to heat the area lightly; the clay pieces will stick.

Melting the wax

You can melt encaustic wax the traditional way in a coffee can on a hot plate, but I used a melting pot made for UTEE (ultra thick embossing powder) set at 250°F (120°C). If the wax starts to smoke, lower the temperature. Liners are available for the melting pot, which are useful for mixing different colors of wax. Cover your work surface with plenty of newspaper and place the clay piece onto a ceramic tile. Wear gloves to protect your hands from hot wax. Work in a well-ventilated area but not in front of a window because the wax cools quickly. Place a lid on the pot to keep it hot. If you mar the surface of the wax, use a heat gun to reheat it and correct the problem.

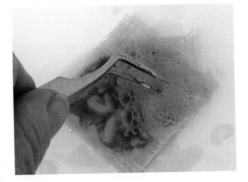

4 Add another small piece of lace, overlapping the other elements of the design in a decorative way.

— Encaustic wax colored with oil paint or mixed with pigments and powders can be used as an embellishment in itself.

5 Try adding a range of other objects to the clay, from chains and beads to dried leaves. A small length of chain is being added here. Submerge the chain in the wax and lay it on the clay as before. Use the tongue depressor to apply more wax over the chain. Heat the decorated tile with the heat gun to smooth down the wax. When cool, trim the edges.

Attaching fabric with liquid clay

1 Liquid clay works like a glue when attaching clay to clay, but it can also be used to glue fabric to clay. The fabric can then be baked in the oven at the low baking temperature of the clay. Pour some liquid clay into a paper cup, add a few drops of mineral oil and mix together. This makes the liquid clay a little easier to spread.

2 Roll out a sheet of clay, ⅛in (3mm) thick, and cut to the required size. Cut out some pieces of fabric. Paint liquid clay onto the clay sheet and lay the first fabric piece on top. Use the paintbrush to press the fabric into the liquid clay. Paint more liquid clay over the top of the fabric until it is completely covered (the fabric will look slightly waxy).

3 Add more liquid clay where you are going to place the next piece of fabric and apply it in the same way. Continue adding fabric until you have completed your design. Cover the whole piece with more liquid clay and then bake. Use scissors to trim any fabric that overhangs the edges.

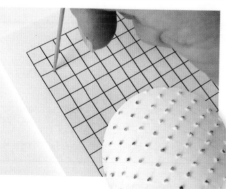

Plotting a grid

1 Press a piece of grid or graph paper onto a sheet of raw clay. Use a sharp needle to pierce a hole through the clay where the lines intersect, then peel the paper off the clay. If you press the paper onto another sheet of clay, the prickings on the paper will mark the grid onto the clay. You can often use the same paper to mark several sheets of clay before the holes go flat.

2 Bake the clay. If the holes are not fully open after baking, poke the needle through to create a clear channel. You can also enlarge the holes using a hand drill. Use the holes for different kinds of embellishments, such as embroidery stitching or beads threaded onto headpins. If adding wire embellishment, take care not to pull the wire too tight or you might cut through the clay.

3 You can use the same technique to mark a grid onto baked clay, but don't try to pierce all the way through the clay. Just press firmly enough to make a mark, then use a hand drill to drill through each mark. The holes should be large enough to accommodate a tapestry needle.

EMBELLISHMENTS

Tile samples

You can embellish your pieces with clay additions or attach a variety of decorative mixed media objects. All sorts of techniques can be used, from sculpting and applying clay shapes to covering the clay with fabric and sewing cross-stitch designs through holes in the clay. Whatever your preference, be it charms and chains or stickers and wax, polymer clay makes the perfect canvas for expressing mixed media ideas.

MIXED MEDIA

1 Accessorize
Materials to be attached (see page 144); champagne clay
How-to: Try out different embedding techniques for attaching a variety of objects to the clay (see page 144). This includes encasing objects between layers of clay, pressing them into the surface and applying clay pieces on top to hold them in place.

2 Framed metal coil
Metal coil; several shades of green clay plus brown
How-to: Thin sheets of clay in several shades of green form a frame around a coiled metal strip from an old watch. The coil is applied to a thicker sheet of brown clay with liquid clay and held in place by the overlapping green layers so that it still "dances" when worn as a brooch. The rough edges of the green layers add texture and visual interest to the design.

"3D greennn" tile by Saskia Veltenaar.

3 Stitch in time
Embroidery threads in several colors; black clay
How-to: Plot a grid on a tile of baked clay and then drill the holes (see page 147). Work embroidery stitches through the grid of holes—here, cross-stitches with a few French knots add embellishment.

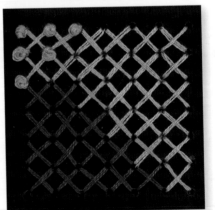

Steampunk goddess brooch
Marie Segal
The elements of the polymer clay goddess—heart bodice, wings and head—are wired onto a handbuilt wire frame. Additional objects are added, including clay flowers, a metal key, watch parts, beads and metal filigree pieces on the wings.

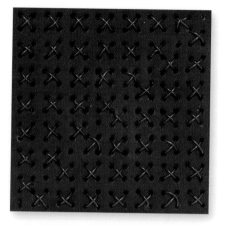

4 Copperpot

Thin copper wire; black clay
How-to: Plot a grid of holes on a sheet of raw clay and then bake (see page 147). Fold the wire in half and thread the ends through two adjacent holes; cross the wires and thread them through to the back through another two holes to form a cross-stitch. Trim the wire neatly at the back. You can also use the holes to attach other decorations, such as beads threaded onto headpins.

7 Cherub and chain

Materials for embedding plus encaustic wax (see page 146); baked white clay tile
How-to: Melt the wax, immerse the objects one at a time into the hot wax and then apply to the baked clay tile. For small items, such as tiny clay shapes, place them onto the tile and then apply melted wax over them. Allow the wax to set.

5 Stuck on you

JeJe peel-off stickers and UV resin; black clay
How-to: Place stickers onto a tile of baked clay. Rub on well to make sure that they are stuck down. These stickers can also be placed onto raw clay and baked in the oven (see page 126). Apply a coat of UV resin and allow to cure.

8 Cherub and leaf

Dried leaf, printed paper napkin, piece of lace and encaustic wax (see page 146); baked gold clay tile
How-to: Make this in the same way as tile 7. Note how the color of the leaf shows through areas of the thin paper cherub.

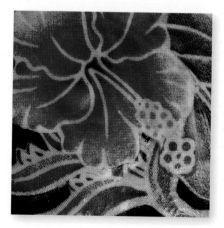

6 Fabric flowers

Fabric with floral motifs and liquid clay; black clay
How-to: Cover a sheet of black clay with liquid clay, lay a fabric motif on top and then apply more liquid clay over the fabric. Continue adding motifs in this way, then bake and trim (see page 147).

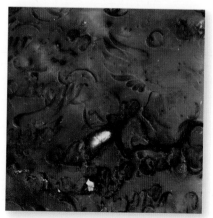

9 Encaustic texture

Encaustic wax, cold wax medium and oil paint; baked tile with deeply textured surface
How-to: Melt encaustic wax and add oil paint to color it (see page 146). Use a tongue depressor to apply it to the tile (the wax will stick better to a deeply textured surface). Use a heat gun to keep the wax liquid. Impress the wax with a texture sheet misted with water. Mix black oil paint into the cold wax medium and use an old towel to rub this onto the tile.

See page 36 for glitter-decorated flower.

APPLIED CLAY

10 Black narcissus
Black clay
How-to: Use cutters to cut out teardrop-shaped leaves and petals. Apply them to a background square of clay, curving the petals over a finger first and finishing with a ball of clay in the center (see page 140). All of the elements are embellished with simple marks.

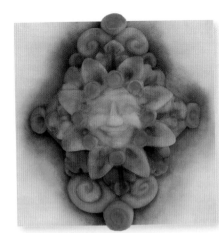

13 Green man
Decorative chalks; flesh-colored clay
How-to: Use a commercial mold to mold a clay face or other motif and apply to a clay sheet. Brush on colored chalks, a little at a time. Chalks are wonderful for enhancing sculptural pieces. A coating of gel medium or liquid clay can be applied to protect the chalk decoration; it will look like a glaze. Chalks can also be mixed into liquid clay as a colorant.

11 Pastel flower
Oil paints in various colors, embossing powder and liquid clay; white clay
How-to: Make this in the same way as tile 10 but using smaller cutters and leaving the petals and center disk flat. Mark the petals with radiating lines and stipple the center with a needle tool. Glaze with colored liquid clay (see page 33), sprinkle black embossing powder onto the stippling and then bake.

14 Steampunk
Opaque and metallic acrylic paints; gold clay
How-to: Impress a pattern into the clay using a variety of tools (chains, ball tools and needle tools), then apply small molded clay shapes to build up a raised design (see page 142). Apply a wash of brown acrylic paint, then wipe off the excess. Highlight areas with metallic acrylic paint.

12 Metallic flower
Mica powder in various colors; black clay
How-to: Make this in the same way as tile 11, but with a smaller flower positioned in one corner; don't stipple the petals. Add thin logs of clay to form curving tendrils and a few small balls as dew drops. Apply mica powders to the raised clay shapes using a small paintbrush or make-up applicator.

15 Landscape window
Gold leaf and UV resin; orange and stardust clay (dark metallic clay with glitter mixed in)
How-to: Apply gold leaf to orange clay and roll to give it a square crackle (see tile 30, page 41). Apply waterslide transfers on top (see page 72). Use a ripple blade to cut strips from stardust clay for the outer frame; texture the strips. Use thin strips of gold leaf clay to define the window panes. Bake, then coat with resin.

Tiles by Madonna Liza Cruz-Comia.

16 Four seasons

Gold leaf, alcohol inks, mica powders and metallic acrylic paints; clay in various colors

How-to: For the background tiles, alcohol inks are applied over textured gold leaf for spring (top left) and winter (bottom right). These contrast strongly with summer (top right) and fall (bottom left), where the inks are applied directly to the clay with areas masked off for a batik effect. Caned and hand-formed leaves are appliquéd onto each tile in a radiating design to reflect the cycle of the seasons, together with additional simple clay shapes. The appliqué pieces are impressed with a variety of marks for additional textural interest. The tiles are finished with mica powders and metallic acrylics.

17 Butterflies and flowers

Rainbow collar cane (see page 89)

How-to: Canes can be formed into all sorts of shapes to create patterned clay embellishments. A multicolored striated cane is used here, but you can use other cane patterns and color palettes in the same way. For the flowers, pinch the cane into a petal shape. Arrange five petal slices on your work surface, press them together, then slice the flower off the work surface and indent the center as you pierce a hole to be used for attachment. For the butterflies, shape one section of cane into an upper wing and another section into a lower wing. Place together, then cut two slices to form a whole butterfly. Add a shaped log in the center for the body and pierce a hole on either side for attachment.

EMBELLISHMENTS

Polymer clay artists at work

Polymer clay lends itself to mixed media, as you can see from the work of these artists, who combine gears, stones, wires, crystals, beads, metal and wood with their clay creations. Polymer clay itself can also be used to create embellishments, from simple clay shapes to using the clay to replicate other objects, such as rocks and plant forms. Make a mold of your embellished pieces so that you can replicate them quickly and easily.

» See pages 148–151 for tile samples

◄ Astraea pendant

Izabela Nowak

Techniques used: The artist's intention with this piece was to create structure rather than pattern. The colorful beads are formed from strips of clay wound into spirals of different sizes. These are attached to a lightweight polymer clay form at the center of the structure using headpins. A small round silver bead is threaded onto each headpin, followed by a spiral bead. The multiple spirals give the pendant texture and visual interest. The pendant measures about 2¾in (7cm) long and 2¾in (7cm) at the widest point.

See MIXED MEDIA tile 1

◄ Seymour wire basket and stand

Marie Segal

Techniques used: Clay petals are attached to a handmade wire basket to give the impression of an otherworldly plant form. Each petal is individually wired onto the basket through holes pierced through the base of the petal. The petals are made in the same way as the rainbow collar on page 89, but using a different color palette and more elongated cane slices. The whole piece stands about 7in (18cm) high.

See MIXED MEDIA tiles 1 & 4

► Blue beauty focal bead

Christi Friesen

Techniques used: This 2½in (6cm) long focal bead in the shape of a seahorse is embellished with clay additions, such as strips of clay wrapped around the eye and tail. These are enhanced by bead and metal additions, especially the vintage watch pieces. The bead for the eye is embedded into the clay and the metal pieces are either embedded into the clay or attached with handmade wire staples. To accentuate the steampunk feel, mica powders are brushed onto the raw clay to imitate metal and after baking the piece is antiqued with acrylic paints.

See MIXED MEDIA tile 1 and APPLIED CLAY tiles 10, 12, 14 & 16

◄▼ Baby sculpture with removable jewelry

Andrea Victoria Paradiso

Techniques used: This 12 x 7 x 6in (30 x 18 x 15cm) sculpture representing the Ace of Cups tarot card is built over a champagne glass. The glass is covered with clay in the form of imitation rocks, with a raised perch where the sea dragon Baby sits holding a crystal in its outstretched hand. Baby's perch is a hinged lid that can be raised to reveal a rock pool filled with colorful sea life in the bowl of the glass (inset picture). When the perch is closed, the removable necklace and earrings (left) become an integral part of the design. As well as the hand-sculpted clay decorations, the piece is embellished with beads, semiprecious stones and wire headpins.

See MIXED MEDIA tile 1 and APPLIED CLAY tiles 10, 12, 14 & 16

▲ Prince of the perch pendant

Christi Friesen

Techniques used: The peacock is handbuilt onto a wire frame, with logs of clay applied to form stylized tail feathers. Small leaves embellish the perch. The bead for the eye is embedded into a small ball of clay and then applied to the head. The beads on the tail and crown are threaded onto headpins for attachment. After baking, acrylic paints are applied to finish the effect.

See MIXED MEDIA tile 1 and APPLIED CLAY tiles 10, 12, 14 & 16

◄ Madonna Liza bangle

Genevieve Q. Montano

Techniques used: A bangle blank is covered with polymer clay and textured, then a commercial mold is used to create the flower embellishments. Additional balls and logs of clay are applied, and the balls are indented with a ball stylus. Acrylic paints are brushed on to imitate patinas, and alcohol inks are used to color the clay further. The bangle is shown from two angles.

See APPLIED CLAY tiles 10, 12, 14 & 16

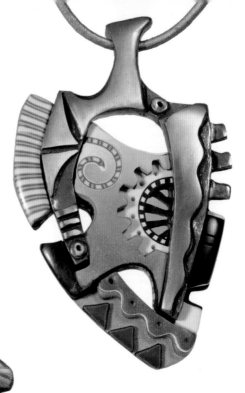

◄ Wooden doll

Meta Strick

Techniques used: This carved wooden doll wears a panel dress made from textured and layered sheets of off-white clay. The center of the dress is decorated with flattened logs and torn-edged strips of clay. Small balls of clay are added on one side of the dress and steel-wired buttons on the other side. The dress is stained with acrylic paint to give it an old and weathered look. The doll measures about 13in (33cm) high and 5in (12.5cm) at the widest part of the dress.

See MIXED MEDIA tiles 1–2 and APPLIED CLAY tiles 10, 12 & 14

◄ Octopus duo pendants

Carissa Nichols

Techniques used: Sculpted amoeba-like forms made out of lightweight clay are colored with alcohol inks dribbled and dropped onto the surface before baking. Swarovski crystals are embedded into pieces of gold clay, which are textured to create decorative bezels. These are attached to the handmade pointed clay bails, which are pierced horizontally for hanging. Each pendant measures 3½ x 2in (9 x 5cm).

See MIXED MEDIA tile 1

► Fantasy island brooch

Ponsawan Sila

Techniques used: A hand-sculpted island is built out of black polymer clay over a wire armature and embellished with simple shapes, including small indented balls of clay, larger clay balls indented to form cup shapes, tapered logs applied vertically and small leaves and flowers. Small cutters can be used to cut out flowers, which can then be cupped to create raised petals. Metallic acrylic paints accentuate the fantasy theme, and rhinestones are embedded for additional sparkle. The brooch measures 4 x 3 x ¾in (10 x 7.5 x 2cm).

See MIXED MEDIA tile 1 and APPLIED CLAY tiles 10, 12 & 14

◄ Pendant

Dawn Stubitsch

Techniques used: This 2¾ x 1¾in (7 x 4.5cm) pendant is a lovely combination of metal clay and polymer clay. The artist starts by making the copper section in metal clay, which forms the anchor around which the polymer clay design is built. Plain and blended colors and simple cane slices are applied to the metal framework, but it is the contrasts of form and space created by the cutaway sections and openings that really carry the piece, creating a complex design that is both organic and geometric.

See MIXED MEDIA tile 1 and APPLIED CLAY tiles 14–15

◄ Orange wreath necklace

Marie Segal

Techniques used: Cane flowers ranging from ½in (13mm) to 1½in (4cm) diameter and in toning shades of orange are pierced with holes in the center for attaching them to a wire framework. The framework is built from thick wire and consists of individual wire arcs joined together. A flower is attached to each arc using finer wire, with carnelian chips threaded onto the center of each wire to hold the flower in place. Small leaves made using the same cane but in shades of green are interspersed between the flowers. The clasp and eye for the closure are hand formed.

See MIXED MEDIA tile 1 and APPLIED CLAY tile 17

◄ Chlorophyll pendant

Daniela D'Uva

Techniques used: Polymer clay leaves are textured by impressing real leaves into the clay surface. The clay leaves are then cut in half and baked over an armature to create their curving shape. Thin wire is used to attach the leaves to the handcrafted wire frame, and a few beads wired onto the frame complete the embellishment. The intertwined wire and clay are in perfect harmony, with the wire forming the central vein of the leaves and curling around them like vine tendrils.

See MIXED MEDIA tiles 1 & 4

◄ Flame shrine

Lindly Haunani

Techniques used: This shrine is built over a 9 x 5 x 4in (23 x 12.5 x 10cm) wooden box. The front of the box is covered with textured strips of polymer clay in blended colors, pieced together like a quilt pattern. The texture is applied by pressing 40-grit sandpaper onto the clay. The wavy side panels of the shrine are formed from square-edged strips of clay. The roof is made from logs of clay rolled into elongated cones. Acrylic beads are attached to the bottom of the shrine for feet.

See APPLIED CLAY tiles 10, 12 & 15–16

Index

Page numbers in *italics* refer to tile samples; page numbers in **bold** refer to finished pieces by polymer clay artists

Clay artists

Credits

Quarto would like to thank all of the polymer clay artists for kindly supplying images of their work for inclusion in this book. Artists are acknowledged beside their work and in the list of clay artists on pages 158–9.

All other images are the copyright of Quarto Publishing plc. While every effort has been made to credit contributors, Quarto would like to apologize should there have been any omissions or errors—and would be pleased to make the appropriate correction for future editions of the book.

Author's acknowledgments

I would like to thank:

- My husband for his support, help and understanding during the conception and completing of this project. Also for his patience and his neverending answer of yes to "Can I have some more of this clay, tool or paint?"
- My editor Michelle for compiling and making sense of a neverending pile of information and photos with no rhyme or reason, that without her brilliance this would still be a neverending pile of information and photos with no rhyme or reason. You have made this enjoyable—it could have been different.
- My dear friend Jodi for helping to expand my mind with new mediums, information and products that I normally wouldn't have thought twice about, which in turn has helped me so much in my polymer work. Your talents are amazing!
- My sweet Susan, for her neverending belief in me and her friendship.
- All of the polymer clay artists whose work is featured in this book for sharing their eye candy—without their talents and inspiration, this wouldn't be such a beautiful work at all.
- The following companies for their support, their wonderful products and their willingness to give me those products whenever I asked:

Art Institute Glitter
- Glitter and fabric glitter glue
- www.artglitter.com

Clay Factory
- Fimo texture sheets, Fimo Classic and Fimo Effects clay, Cernit clay, Kemper tools and cutters, and Makin's Clay products
- www.clayfactory.net

Clearsnap
- Archival ink
- www.clearsnap.com

Environmental Technology
- EasyMold two-part putty silicone molding compound, resin and support
- www.eti-usa.com

ERA Graphics
- Unmounted rubber stamps
- www.eragraphics.com

Jacquard Products
- Cernit clay, brushes, Lumiere and Neopaque acrylic paints, encaustic wax medium, Dorland's wax medium, Pearl Ex powders and lacquer, Piñata alcohol inks and support
- www.jacquardproducts.com

Katy Sue Designs Limited
- Flower Soft, molds and paper images
- www.flower-soft.com

Kool Tak
- Transfer foils and embellishment pick-up pencils
- www.stix2kooltakusa.com

Lisa Liddy at Metal Me This
- Metal coatings and patinas
- www.etsy.com/shop/metalmethis

Makin's Clay Company USA
- Shape cutters, texture sheets, Ultimate clay extruder, Ultimate clay machine and support
- www.makins-usa.com

Rubber Stamp Plantation
- Mounted rubber stamps
- www.rubberstampplantation.com

Sparkraft Enterprises
- JeJe stickers
- www.sparkraftent.com

Staedtler
- Fimo Classic and Fimo Effects clay, Fimo Liquid Deco Gel, Lumocolor pens and support
- www.staedtler.ca

Viva Decor
- Glass-effect gel
- www.viva-decor.us